T0330105

MANAGEMENT FUNDAMENTALS

MANAGEMENT FUNDAMENTALS

STEVEN COHEN
AND WILLIAM EIMICKE

COLUMBIA UNIVERSITY PRESS | NEW YORK

Columbia University Press

Publishers Since 1893

New York   Chichester, West Sussex

cup.columbia.edu

Copyright © 2020 Columbia University Press

All rights reserved

Library of Congress Cataloging-in-Publication Data

Names: Cohen, Steven, 1953 September 6- author. | Eimicke,
William B., author.

Title: Management fundamentals / Steven Cohen and William Eimicke.

Description: New York : Columbia University Press, 2020. | Includes
bibliographical references and index.

Identifiers: LCCN 2020000811 (print) | LCCN 2020000812 (ebook) |
ISBN 9780231194488 (hardback) | ISBN 9780231194495
(trade paperback) | ISBN 9780231550857 (ebook)

Subjects: LCSH: Management.

Classification: LCC HD31.2 .C636 2020 (print) | LCC HD31.2
(ebook) | DDC 658—dc23

LC record available at https://lccn.loc.gov/2020000811

LC ebook record available at https://lccn.loc.gov/2020000812

Cover design: Noah Arlow

To Marvin, Shirley, and Lily—the past and the future.
And to Karen, Annemarie, and Sugar Ray—good
things come in threes.

CONTENTS

CONTENTS

MANAGEMENT FUNDAMENTALS

INTRODUCTION

Organizational management is a widely misunderstood activity that many of us, at one time or another, have experienced, exercised, or maybe even fallen victim to. In modern media, management has been depicted with humor (think of the pointy-haired boss in the cartoon *Dilbert*); provided entertainment (as in the reality show *The Apprentice*); and inspired (such as through a news story about a fire chief leading a crew into a burning building and saving a family).

This book is a primer on the fundamental elements of management—a periodic table for the field, if you will. As such, *Management Fundamentals* surveys the basic responsibilities of managing organizations and examines the general role of the manager, dividing their work into three main areas of practice:

1. **Operation.** Ensuring the organization runs smoothly and effectively and engages with the environment to generate resources.
2. **Opportunity.** Taking advantage of open doors and protecting the organization from attack.
3. **Organization in society.** Shaping the organization's place in society, which includes managing stakeholder relations,

politics, and ethical standards, and preparing for the future of work itself. As work changes, the role of the manager changes as well.

This book defines the practices and concepts that comprise modern management and define contemporary managers. We avoid contemporary examples, however; instead, we identify and explain the broader essential elements of management, creating a roadmap for new managers and a reference tool for experienced ones. To do so, we ask and answer these seven questions:

1. What are the fundamental elements of the work of management and managers?
2. What tools and techniques can they employ as they do the work of management?
3. How does a manager ensure that the organization he or she manages generates enough resources to survive and thrive?
4. How does a manager ensure that the organization develops and maintains functional relationships with customers, clients, and stakeholders?
5. How can a manager maintain personal integrity—and the integrity of his or her organization?
6. How has the modern technological world and global economy changed the work of managers?
7. What is the future of work and its management?

Management Fundamentals builds on our decades of experience as managers and management professors, combining what we have learned both in practice and in the literature about effective management. Further, it is a management book for organizations and managers in all three sectors: public, private, and nonprofit. We do not assume a profit motive, a public purpose, or a mission-orientation—instead, we write as if all three motivations are in play. Each chapter focuses on a key element of effective management. The first chapter defines management and looks at the major trends in management, beginning with those in the early twentieth century. We discuss how Taylorism and the Hawthorne Experiments influenced the basics of management and the trends that followed. While these theories were advancing, four major developments simultaneously defined modern management: accounting, computing and low-cost communication, the global economy and global supply chains, and sustainability.

Why these four developments? Financial management and low-cost communication made modern organizational networks and cross-sector partnerships possible. Physical proximity is no longer a prerequisite for management influence and control, enabling global supply chains and new ways of accomplishing organizational goals. On a more crowded, resource constrained planet, an organization's cost structure is dramatically impacted by its energy bills and its production of pollution and waste. Sustainable practices are not only essential for stemming climate change and creating a healthier environment, but as an organization saves energy, reduces pollution, and minimizes waste, it significantly improves its bottom line. While management continues to evolve, the basic concepts of management persist. The rest of the chapter outlines and describes these concepts.

The second chapter begins with leadership within management, drawing upon Selznick's theory of the "Role of the Leader" to show where leaders fit in an organization. This discussion is followed by a section on decision-making: it outlines the ideal process for decision-making and looks at how managers can make better decisions by using tools to avoid mistakes and enhance the probability of success. The chapter then moves on to organizational communication and how to build an internal communication strategy. Finally, the last section focuses on risk management, defining what risk is, why managers should worry about risk and uncertainty, and how they can identify, evaluate, and manage risks.

Money is the single most important tool a manager has to influence an organization's behavior and is a sure way of tracking organizational priorities and activities. For this reason, in the third chapter, we explore budgets and financial management, defining and discussing the different types of budgets used by organizations. We also explore financial management or control systems and how they can influence behavior.

Chapter 4 covers human resource management, organizational structure, and standard operating procedures. In human resource management, we look at the centrality of influencing, motivating, and coordinating people's work. How can one find and hire excellent staff, motivate staff, and deal with inadequate staff? Next, we outline organizational structure and analyze how it can help managers manage. We also consider the limits of this tool and discuss when a manager should or should not use it. In the area of standard operating procedures, we examine how work is performed in reporting relationships according to organizational norms and routines. Leaders and senior managers may not do this work directly, but they must set guidelines on how this work should be done and then track and evaluate how well it is being done. As such, we discuss how work gets designed, completed, and changed over time.

The fifth chapter defines performance management and builds on the ideas of management theorist Peter Drucker. We delve into the essentials of performance management (benchmarking, measuring success, and accountability) and the four categories of performance measures (input indicators, process indicators, outputs, and outcome). We discuss information management by looking at the role of data and how it can help managers. We then conclude by detailing how to successfully use performance management.

In chapter 6 we explore sustainability: its feasibility, prerequisites, and challenges. We discuss technical impediments to sustainability—such as a lack of technology or insufficient knowledge to implement technology—and show managers how to adopt technology to the benefit of the organization. We also examine the political challenges of sustainability, which include short-term thinking, compared with the long-term thinking required for sustainability.

Chapter 7 looks at strategic planning and how it can be used within an organization successfully. Managers must know how to develop a strategy, implement it, and understand its costs and benefits; as such, this chapter details the seven elements of strategy and demonstrates why an organization needs one.

After outlining why contract management is important, chapter 8 explains the central elements of contract management and outlines what managers need to know to manage contracts. We examine the obstacles to contracting and how to overcome them. We discuss why managers should and should not contract out and the role of the make-or-buy decision. The chapter concludes by looking at the future of contracting. We have written an entire book on this topic (*The Responsible Contract Manager*), and in this chapter we reduce those three hundred pages to about ten.

To improve performance, chapter 9 analyzes and describe partnerships across sectors. These are often called Private-Public Partnerships (PPPs) and more recently include Cross-Sector

Partnerships (CSPs). Here, we answer the questions: Why is it important to partner with other organizations? And what makes a partnership successful?

Chapter 10 considers how managers can use marketing, stakeholder relations, and public engagement to their advantage. We begin by crafting an effective marketing strategy, and then we examine stakeholder relations and how different stakeholders influence a manager's position. We also discuss how stakeholders can be leveraged in different situations. Finally, we explain the ins and outs of public engagement and why it is essential.

In chapter 11, we explore the origin of organizational ethics. Scholars like Carol Lewis believe that public ethics are different from personal ethics. In the public realm, ethics are comprised of action-based judgments of right and wrong. Managers must deal with various ethical issues, and this chapter analyzes the central ones they now face—and how to resolve them.

The final chapter looks to the future of work. Technology, culture, and social norms are changing the nature of work and, thus, changing what happens during the workday and how managers respond to challenges. For example, with technological capabilities that now enable people to work 24/7, how can managers help employees find a work-life balance that retains talent and prevents burnout?

Our effort here is to present the management concepts that we consider absolutely critical. We had to make very difficult choices when deciding what to include and what to omit from this work. We deliberately provide an overview that we believe provides the fundamental practices and concepts of management in clear and practical terms. We believe that a manager who reads and utilizes this book will be a better and more effective manager.

1

THE EVOLUTION OF MANAGEMENT

Over the past century, the field of management has evolved largely in response to changes in technology, society, and economic life. We can trace this evolution through landmark books that defined the management styles of their eras. At the start of the twentieth century, we saw the development of mass production and, in response, the rise of a management theory called Taylorism, which saw people as extensions of the assembly line. Fredrick Winslow Taylor's influential book *The Principles of Scientific Management* brought us time and motion studies, which attempted to measure individual work and output and maximize production.[1] Under Taylorism, management was straightforward: managers defined work and designed tasks, and workers did whatever management told them.[2] Teamwork and individual creativity were not part of this management approach. Taylor's focus on designing, rationalizing, and improving work processes would have lasting effects, leading ultimately to the management theories of W. Edwards Deming. Deming was a statistician, management consultant, and professor at New York University. After World War II, he guided Japanese businesses in reforming management and rebuilding Japan's economy.[3] He championed his theory of Total Quality Management, in which workers participated in the design of tasks. This was a departure from Taylor's strategies, which held no interest in views and information offered by workers.[4]

In between Taylor and Denning, from 1924 to 1932, a man named Elton Mayo conducted the Hawthorne experiments, largely undertaken at the Western Electric plant in Cicero, Illinois. The Hawthorne experiments originally set out to test whether brighter lighting would increase productivity on the assembly line. The findings varied, but during the testing process, researchers realized that an array of human factors—supervision and competition among them—could influence productivity. The resulting human relations school of management came to focus on the social psychology of the workplace, including worker motivation, which researchers found to arise from group dynamics and processes and from communication between management and workers.[5]

Shortly after Mayo's findings gained prominence, Chester Barnard, a corporation president in the 1920s and 1930s, published his pathbreaking (if somewhat boring) work, *Functions of the Executive*.[6] In it, Barnard theorized that an organization organically obtained work by providing incentives, which he, in turn, developed a typology for. He also highlighted the importance of communication, cohesion, cooperation, and what he identified as "informal organization"—effective organizational operations that spring from informal social networks. Such networks, according to Barnard, develop via social interactions that occur during group work and after-work activities, which then give way to informal patterns of communication that do not adhere to a formal hierarchical structure.

Building on Barnard, Phillip Selznick's 1957 book *Leadership in Administration* examined the evolution of individual perceptions of organizations.[7] To Selznick, an organization's member first sees the organization in Taylor-like terms: as a neutral piece of machinery. Over time, the member grows to view the organization differently, seeing it as what Selznick termed "an institution." An institution is valued by its members for what it *is* as much as for what it does. In an institution, individuals can achieve self-actualization, and their loyalty and emotional attachment to the organization grow.

Peter Drucker's *Concept of the Corporation* (1946) and *Practice of Management* (1954) conceptualized the organization as a social system, focusing on the elements of organizational life that lead to organizational productivity.[8] Similarly, Deming saw the organization as a social system but as one focused on the production of work. By defining quality in terms of customer preferences, Deming sought to focus workers on producing what customers wanted with as little waste as possible. Using worker participation and performance statistics, he drove waste from production processes, reducing errors and increasing quality. From the standpoint of management theory, he combined the emphasis on the organization as a social system with the process of work.

Finally, two management consultants, Thomas J. Peters and Robert H. Waterman, in their 1982 best-seller *In Search of Excellence*, complemented Deming's analytical approach with their own, which emphasized the behavior of managers in developing and nurturing productive social systems.[9] Urging managers to get out from behind their desks and to engage with the organization, Peters and Waterman advocated what they called "Management by Wandering Around."[10] We doubt Deming would have appreciated the randomness of the approach, but the effort to connect with the organization's social system would have been understood by Mayo, Drucker, Barnard, and Selznick—and, maybe even Deming.

THE EVOLUTION OF MANAGEMENT FUNDAMENTALS

Four developments in the twentieth and early twenty-first centuries had major effects on management theory and practice: the establishment of the Generally Accepted Accounting Practices (GAAP), the introduction of computing (and the resulting lowered cost of communication), the growth of the global economy and global supply chains, and the addition of physical dimensions of sustainability as a major management responsibility.

ACCOUNTING

In many respects, the field of accounting emerged from the Great Depression in the United States. There were many causes for the stock market crash of 1929—"on margin" stock trading (paying only some of the cost of the stock and borrowing money to pay the rest), insider trading, and a host of related issues—but one fundamental problem was that companies selling shares on public stock exchanges were not honestly or accurately reporting their finances. An investor could not tell if a company was making or losing money. This changed under the New Deal, when the Security and Exchange Commission (SEC) was established to regulate the public marketplace for company shares.[11] President Franklin Delano Roosevelt appointed Joseph P. Kennedy, a well-known Wall Street speculator and the father of President John F. Kennedy, as the first head of the SEC. [12]

THE EVOLUTION OF MANAGEMENT

The SEC required companies offering stock to the public to adhere to a set of accounting principles, which came to be known as Generally Accepted Accounting Principles, or GAAP. Under GAAP, investors could learn the true financial conditions of companies they were considering investing in via access to those companies' financial reports—reports audited by certified accounting firms.[13] The stock market would never be risk-free, but with GAAP, it no longer resembled a casino, as it had in the 1920s.

The development of GAAP meant that organizations now periodically had to meet or exceed financial targets, which had to be expressed in the specific terminology of accounting. As such, managers had to learn the basics of accounting. Before, a manager needed to be concerned with production, logistics, marketing, and sales, but now financial management and the effective use of capital were added to that list.

In addition, the concept of finance changed. Before GAAP, finance tended to be limited to amassing capital for production and counting revenues and profits. After GAAP, however, organizations were required to monitor more detailed financial information, and as such, these organizations were also managed to achieve specific financial targets.[14]

As a result, the public sector saw the growth of the municipal bond market. In the nonprofit sector, endowments and borrowing for capital expenditures, such as new facilities, increased. And in the private sector, shareholders expected return from the equity they invested in a company in the form of higher stock prices or dividends.

INFORMATION MANAGEMENT

New accounting practices brought financial information to the forefront of the manager mindset, but computing and low-cost communication led managers to look at nonfinancial indicators of organizational performance. Organizational inputs, work processes, outputs, and outcomes could now be quickly measured by workers and reported to management. Monthly reports became weekly reports and then daily reports. By the end of the twentieth century, managers could receive real-time data on organizational performance and see the effects of their decisions. New reports and data allowed for a granular calibration of organizational activities.[15] Unfortunately, they also increased the short-sightedness of managers, since immediate actions and results were easy to understand. Thus, management came to focus primarily on what it could measure, and what gets measured not only gets done but also continues to be focused on. The noise made by short-term indicators has made it nearly impossible to implement strategies that take a long time to achieve.[16]

The allure of real-time results, however, continues to prove irresistible to contemporary managers. In fact, the modern manager is typically an information junkie, seeking to understand all aspects of organizational performance in order to reduce uncertainty and increase the probability of achieving organizational goals. The performance indicators they receive are often reported in real time on electronic "dashboards," creating a more fact-based form of management, but this can easily result in information overload. Managers must distinguish more important indicators from less important ones and still interpret and analyze the information collected.[17] For this reason, the proliferation of management indicators and the use of data to identify and justify management priorities have become characteristic of modern organizational life.

THE GLOBAL ECONOMY, NETWORK MANAGEMENT, AND GLOBAL SUPPLY CHAINS

Technology radically altered the world of management not only by making inexpensive information more accessible but also by altering the production process. New technologies such as cellular communication, cheap computing, bar codes, and GPS meant that companies that once produced many components of a piece of manufactured equipment and owned the vehicles to ship them were now buying components from suppliers who, in turn, shipped the components in vehicles owned by shipping companies. The resulting supply chains—in which supplies are produced in many locations and then shipped far and wide to be assembled—now sometimes stretch around the globe.

Manufacturers can thus forgo maintaining huge, costly inventories in warehouses adjacent to their production lines and instead use just-in-time shipping, where supplies arrive shortly before they are used.[18] A supply can be tracked from the moment it leaves one factory to the moment it enters another. Huge quantities of goods can be shipped in containers lifted by cranes off of ships and placed directly on trains and trucks for transport.

We can see the same networked production processes in manufacturing and service industries. Call centers in India answer questions from Americans about goods made in China. A website designed and produced in one location has its content written and revised in another and features videos made in various cities. Service providers like universities and hospitals outsource food service, building maintenance, and even accounting and human resources.

These new production processes mean organizations have become more specialized. One company can specialize in making smartphone screens and another in batteries. The people who design the phones are not the same people who assemble them.[19] This greater specialization has made it possible for huge, vertically integrated bureaucracies governed by formal, hierarchical organizational structures to be largely replaced by more horizontally structured, "flatter" networks of smaller organizations.[20]

Further, an increasing portion of management's work is focused on contract management at a global scale.[21] Managers must somehow influence the behavior of people who do not directly work for them or their organization. The motivational lessons of the human relations school of management are not as useful to managers who must obtain work from outside organizations and people in other countries and cultures. Managers must understand national law, culture, economies, and political processes and have the ability to build relationships across organizations and geography.[22]

SUSTAINABILITY

In today's more crowded and observed planet, an organization's use of resources and impact on the planet are now central rather than peripheral management challenges, creating critical issues around cost, reputation, and liability that managers cannot afford to ignore.[23] Where once waste and pollution were considered an expected byproduct of organizational life, the modern organization no longer has the latitude to behave without discipline.

In many respects, twenty-first-century leaders and managers must become as familiar with the tools of sustainability as they are with marketing, finance, strategy, and communication. Managers must understand and act on matters such as energy and water efficiency, renewable energy, materials management, waste management, and the environmental impact of production and consumption. This means that besides understanding organizations, information, communication, production processes, national cultures, finance, and accounting, a manager must also achieve sufficient scientific literacy to engage with scientists, architects, and engineers who are experts in the physical dimensions of sustainability, or hire someone who has this literacy to assist them.

And this requisite care and rigor is not limited to the physical environment. As today's organizations are expected to provide fair and equal treatment to staff regardless of race, gender, sexual orientation, religion, and nation of origin and as rules on permissible social interactions between managers and staff evolved, managers must also lead on changes to the social environment.

CONCLUSION

By necessity, organizational management becomes more complex as the world becomes more complex. But although management evolves over time, some fundamental management concepts remain constant. This book will summarize those concepts, starting with a definition of management.

Management is the art and craft of getting people to work. All things being equal, most of us would rather be sitting on a beach watching the waves or on a couch watching television.

Something gets us to move from that place of rest or recreation to a place of work. That something is motivation.

Managers must motivate workers to work, but work is not a simple, singular thing. Effective management is getting people to do the *right work* in order to meet the organization's goals. To do so, a manager must seek answers from within the organization or (more and more) from the organizational network with which the organization has contractual relations. The manager must honestly assess the organization's capacity, think strategically to set meaningful goals, and then determine the key tasks that must be performed to achieve those goals.[24]

Further, motivating others to work requires managers to offer incentives. The effectiveness of incentives varies by task, by person, and over time. Material reward may be sufficient to motivate some, but others require more, such as a sense of mission or the opportunity to achieve self-actualization. Managers must remember that organizations are not abstractions; they are made of people, and people matter.

Incentives, in turn, require resources, which come from various places outside the organization. First, resources come from the organization's customers, clients, or stakeholders. As a colleague, Ron Brand, used to say, "There are no cash registers in HQ." In other words, all the cash registers are in the store: that is where the customers are, and that is where resources will be uncovered. Second, as Phillip Selznick has said, to obtain resources, an organization must do something no one else can; that is, it must occupy some unique niche.[25] For example, Columbia is the only comprehensive Ivy League university in New York City. And the pizza place on Amsterdam Avenue and 120th Street is the only place to get a slice of pizza within about a third of a mile of its store. To support the organization's effort to obtain resources, management must ensure that basic organizational functions—human resources, procurement, finance, information, facilities, sustainability, strategy, external relations, and marketing—are carried out and coordinated. Management must also ensure organizational maintenance in order to continue attracting and generating the resources an organization needs to survive. As organic entities, all organizations seek to survive. Survival requires resources, and as such, organizations are always about doing the work required to generate and attract resources. This means understanding an organization's capacities and environment, both of which can change. Organizational maintenance means understanding the dynamics and outcomes of any such change and ultimately knowing how to adapt.

PART I

LEADING AND MANAGING ORGANIZATIONAL OPERATIONS

2

LEADERSHIP

Leading and managing are two sides of the same coin—different but directly connected. You can lead without managing and manage without leading, but an organization needs both strong leadership and good management to succeed. Leaders with management skills and managers who can lead are more effective than leaders and managers without at least some of both skillsets.

Why study leadership? A leader influences organizational performance—a change in leadership is often associated with improvement or decline in overall performance measures. Leadership is seldom the only factor in an organization's outcomes, but it can be the most important. It is fortunate, then, that the skills and functions leadership requires can be learned. Leaders are not born; they are made.

Managers and frontline workers alike can become more effective by learning leadership skills. And since leadership is best understood through the relationship between leaders and their followers, learning about leadership can make you a more effective professional, regardless of your position in the organizational hierarchy.

THE LITERATURE OF LEADERSHIP

German sociologist Max Weber is best known for his writings on bureaucracy, but his theories on leadership were just as revolutionary. Weber identified three sources of *legitimate rule,* or what we might simply call *power.*[1] *Traditional authority* arises from one's role in society—for example, as a parent, tribal or community leader, or religious advisor—and roles themselves arise from social and community norms.[2]

Rational or legal authority comes from an organizational bureaucracy, whether political, religious, or civil.[3] Powers are defined by laws, rules, regulations, and processes and then vested in a position of authority. In large, complex organizations, power, authority, and limits are typically specified in an official position description.

Finally, Weber describes *charismatic authority* as arising from an ability to speak well, a clear vision, the words and emotions to inspire, a sense of humanity, and identification with followers.[4] The idea of charisma appears frequently in literature and discussions of power and leadership throughout the world. Often, we hear it described as some kind of magical presence or "star power." In fact, much of the early literature on leadership focused on the Great Man theory, which said that leadership was a native trait and not learned—and that it largely flowed from a mystical attribute known as charisma.[5] But Weber describes charisma as flowing from more concrete attributes, such as having a strategic plan, communication skills, and a relationship with followers based on a sense of mutuality.[6]

Another influential author—and probably the most widely read author on management in the twentieth century—was Peter Drucker. He viewed integrity as the essential element in

effective leadership. Drucker felt that the most important organizational relationship was that between leaders and their followers, and he stressed the importance of leaders learning
people's strengths before helping them develop their capacities
and vision. As a model for encouraging leaders to value their
followers, he quoted famous industrialist Andrew Carnegie's
self-chosen tombstone epitaph: "Here lies a man who knew
how to enlist in his service better men than himself." Drucker
also urged leaders to define a basic social purpose that followers could believe in and strive toward.[7]

At the core of Drucker's definition of effective leadership
and management was the measurement of organizational performance. The leader must have a strategic plan with clear goals
and objectives by which he or she can measure performance.
Data must be collected and judged through indicators that assess the degree to which the goals and objectives were met. And
some risk must be taken to assure performance.[8]

In line with the above philosophies, Drucker believed that
strong leaders must master four basic skills—listening, communicating, paying attention to tasks (rather than to oneself),
and relentlessly focusing on reengineering mistakes.[9]

Similar to Drucker, political scientist James MacGregor
Burns valued the leader-follower relationship. In 1978,
Burns won the Pulitzer Prize and the National Book Award
for his work titled *Leadership,* which the *New York Times*
called "the seminal book on power." In it, Burns argued
that power and leadership should be considered together as
a relationship.[10] According to Burns, leadership is insepara-
ble from followers' needs and goals and will always take one of
two forms: *Transactional leadership* is based on a bargain
where leader and followers exchange valued things—votes for
jobs, for example, or a bonus in return for an increase in sales

volume.[11] *Transformational leadership* is when leaders engage followers in such a way that it raises them all up to a higher level of motivation and morality.[12] The famous question asked by President John F. Kennedy's 1961 inaugural address—"Ask not what your country can do for you; ask what you can do for your country"—effectively illustrates the essence of transformational leadership. President Abraham Lincoln used both transactional and transformational methods.[13] He inspired others with the Emancipation Proclamation, but the transactional need for African Americans to side with the Union motivated the timing of the declaration.

Finally, Warren Bennis, who authored thirty books on leadership, argued that leadership was only one of the functions of management. He identified four strategies of effective leaders, which echo much of what Weber, Drucker, and Burns believed. To Bennis, the first and most critical strategy of successful leadership was having a clearly articulated vision and sense of direction. Second to that, leaders must possess integrity and trustworthiness. Third, leaders must shape and communicate the organization's culture—its values, principles, role models, and sense of meaning. Fourth, contrary to the idea that leadership is primarily about the exercise of power, Bennis argued that leaders must empower *others*, and then translate intentions into reality and sustain that reality. Bennis's collaborative leadership is essential to cross-sector partnerships—and to all management strategy in the twenty-first century.[14] Simply put, he said, "Leaders have a bias toward action that results in success."[15]

LEADERSHIP AS A JOB

Leaders have primary responsibility for the organization's relationship with its external environment. If managers are responsible for making the trains run on time, safely, and at the lowest possible cost, then leaders are responsible for obtaining the resources to make that happen—determining where the trains originate and where they arrive, making sure potential customers know the service is available, and ensuring everyone knows why the train is important. Leaders are also responsible for the future—determining when high-speed rail will be feasible, affordable, and safe—and transitioning the organization to the new reality while maintaining excellent service in the interim.

In a nutshell, successful leaders develop the organization's ideology and values; they develop a vision for the future and create a strategic plan to get there; they recruit and strategically deploy the best and brightest personnel; and they make the decisions required to enable the organization to achieve the best performance possible. Leaders are also essential to the formation and the successful execution of partnerships with other organizations—as such collaborations are often necessary to overcome major challenges and achieve complex objectives and tasks.

What activities must they engage in to successfully execute these responsibilities? Leaders must master financial management to ensure the organization has the resources needed to accomplish its strategic objectives. They must set priorities based on careful analysis, which is usually the product of participatory strategic planning. And they must develop a performance management system to regularly measure key indicators of organizational success.

What skills must leaders master to execute these activities effectively? Leaders must become experts in communication, which includes listening, speaking, and writing. They must understand how to motivate their people to achieve their highest potential; equally important, they must be willing and able to hold their people accountable.

Leaders must initiate change and innovate when circumstances dictate. In many respects, leadership is often associated with managing crises, which, incidentally, often precipitate change and innovation. Change is seldom welcomed by people at work, generally because they worry about their ability to do new things and, therefore, fear their jobs may be in jeopardy. Change and innovation is particularly difficult in large, complex bureaucracies, which are designed to be consistent and complete the same procedures in the same way. In many respects, organizations can be seen as collections of standard operating procedures, and leaders must ensure that these standard procedures are modified to meet new conditions and changing needs. As such, new leaders are often tasked with innovating, which can be particularly challenging if they are new to the organization and its personnel.

As cross-sector partnerships become more common, leaders must also learn to lead in a collaborative fashion. Leaders are more effective in partnership situations when they are able to identify and understand the leadership skills of their counterparts.

HOW CAN LEADERS MOTIVATE FOLLOWERS?

Most leaders have an array of "carrots" and "sticks." A carrot might be a cash bonus or stock options; a performance incentive or promotion; a bigger office, flexible hours, or a work-from-home option; the use of a car, computer, or smart phone; or time off, travel, or childcare. Offering a carrot is what James MacGregor Burns would characterize as transactional leadership. Sticks, on the other hand, might include verbal warnings and threats, lower-than-average pay increases, no pay increase, demotions, undesirable assignments, loss of office space, long hours, and, ultimately, dismissal.

In government-sector jobs and in many large publicly traded private companies, the carrots and sticks available to employers are limited by the civil service, human resource policies, unions, and laws and regulations governed by fair labor practices. And in any case, it would be impossible to continuously dole out rewards and punishments to motivate an entire organization over the long term. A more feasible way to motivate people is to practice what Burns calls *transformational leadership*: inspiring workers with a positive vision for the future.[16] Ideally, a leader will present this vision with passion and reinforce it through his or her everyday actions.

Survey research shows that employees self-report valuing *actions* more than traditional incentives and disincentives. For example, employees frequently rate the following as highly motivating:

- A sense of achievement
- Recognition by superiors
- Enjoyment in their assigned work
- Responsibility for executing important work for the organization
- A reasonable expectation that they will be promoted if they continue to perform well.[17]

Every one of these motivational tools (except, perhaps, for future advancement) are available to a leader at little or no financial cost. Simply put, leaders can motivate employees by making it clear to them that they are important, that their work is important, and that they are doing a good job. As such, effective leaders find the time to make sure that everyone in their organization feels important. They know that success is a team effort, where everyone's work is appreciated and valued.

A more formal and quantifiable way of motivating an entire organization is through a performance management system, which we discuss in more detail in chapter 5. Performance management is a mechanism to hold people accountable for carrying out their duties both internally (for the organization) and externally (for the stakeholders—particularly, customers).

HOW DO LEADERS HOLD PEOPLE ACCOUNTABLE?

Peter Drucker said that the essence of leadership is organizational performance. For an organization to perform well, everyone in the organization must do their part. That's why holding people accountable for doing their jobs well is a key responsibility of leadership.

As mentioned, a performance management system is one way to hold people accountable. It does so by enabling a manager, first, to quantify the outputs and outcomes of the entire organization and its major departments and then, second, to translate those measurements to the performance of each employee. Applying organizational metrics to individual performance, however, can be difficult, because a lot of work requires teams, complex multistep processes, and even contractors and partners from other organizations. In larger, more complicated organizations, it is especially difficult to directly link individual performance to the accomplishment of the organization's key objectives.

That said, the first step in creating true accountability for each member is to develop individualized, detailed job descriptions. People must have a clear, operational knowledge of exactly what they are supposed to do. It may sound obvious and easy, but many job descriptions are vague and can be inaccurate.

Second, leaders must encourage employers to hire the best people available for every position. Politics and personal relationships inevitably come into play during the hiring process; however, successful leaders never forget that an organization is only as good as the people it hires. They know that short-term favors can have a long-term negative impact on an organization's capacity to implement its mission and achieve its goals.

Third, effective leaders invest in ongoing training. This includes providing simulations and exercises to make certain every member of the organization has the knowledge and experience necessary to perform at their highest level, particularly in times of peak demand or crisis. It also includes employing a sufficient number of supervisors who are on board with such training and have the discretion necessary to keep their teams properly focused and synchronized to the organization's goals.

In this same vein, to ensure accountability, many organizations conduct annual performance appraisals, by which supervisors evaluate employees according to predetermined and mutually agreed upon standards. A supervisor provides a written evaluation to each employee, which they then discuss in person. Often, employees are scored on a five-point scale that includes ratings such as outstanding, very good, good, below average, and poor. After discussing the performance assessment, both parties typically sign the document along with an associated agreement of goals for the employee to meet in the year ahead. Typically, a formal appeal process is provided to address disagreements over goals or achievements.

Unfortunately, such appraisal systems cost time and have limited value given the personal dynamics between employees and their direct supervisors: Neither side is usually interested in spending the time and energy required to engage in a detailed and honest evaluation. And for the supervisor, differentiating among direct reports can be personally uncomfortable—it can create hard feelings and is especially difficult when face-to-face discussion is part of the process. Therefore, the vast majority of employees are evaluated as outstanding or no worse than very good.

The value of appraisal systems is further diminished by the reality that they seldom carry direct consequences—whether positive (a raise or promotion) or negative (discipline or termination). In addition, formal management reviews of staff are often influenced or limited by unions, government laws, regulations around labor relations, and collectively bargained contracts. We also see pay increases and promotions governed by civil service or human resources rules in private and nonprofit organizations. That is why rewards given for team, unit, division, or even organization-wide performance are often more useful than individual assessment systems.

Also remember that while effective leaders focus primarily on measuring their organization's outputs and outcomes, they must also ensure that that their members treat their customers, clients, partners, contractors, and external stakeholders with courtesy and respect. As such, one effective way to evaluate employees for accountability purposes is in regard to their customer service. Customer service can be measured through surveys at the point of contact, through follow-up emails to clients, or through customer call centers with a toll-free telephone number.

Leaders can also pursue such feedback more aggressively by hiring contract employees or firms to pose as regular customers, either in person or electronically. Known in the retail business as "secret shoppers," these contractors can offer leaders an effective, if expensive, way to objectively learn how the organization is treating customers.

DEVELOPING YOUR LEADERSHIP SKILLS

Effective leaders recognize the skills and assets that will empower them to improve their organization's performance—and then work on developing those assets. Although the particular skills that a given manager needs can vary based on the organization, some basic assets are prerequisite to any good leader.

First, *intellectual capacity* helps a leader understand complex processes, technology, engineering, human psychology, data analytics, and the many other complexities that contribute to organizational success. When needing to choose from among the strategic options available to an organization, managers who have intellectual capital typically make better decisions. Intellect and knowledge also increase a leader's credibility and influence within the organization and with suppliers, customers, and stakeholders.

A robust professional network of colleagues, political allies, financial and social elites, and friends and family can benefit a leader via association with important societal interests, beliefs, ethnicities, or geographies, either directly or by inference. It can also enable a leader to more effectively influence public opinion, stakeholders, and the legislative and regulatory process, and to form additional beneficial partnerships and alliances. Relatedly, a reputation for success in the field that the organization operates under can also enhance a leader's power, both internally and externally.

Thirdly, Burns argued that effective leaders use *transactional and inspirational skills* to align and motivate followers to achieve their strategic goals. According to him, transactional skills encompass negotiating with followers, stakeholders, and even opponents and competitors, leveraging the resources under your control to achieve the desired outcome.[18] Inspirational skills involve articulating to employees a grand vision for the future, creating trusting relationships with them, and then having the confidence that their collective resources and effort will achieve that grand vision.[19]

Finally, leaders operating within a partnership must master the *skills of convening, coordinating, and catalyzing.* Convening is the ability to identify the particular advantage your organization brings to the partnership—financial resources, prestige, track record, or power—which makes partners and other stakeholders eager to have you lead in developing a comprehensive strategy for success. Coordination is the expertise to direct the distinct efforts of partners into a smooth, reinforcing effort toward your goals. Catalyzing is initiating collective action throughout the partnership, keeping all members engaged and energized in a unified commitment.[20]

LEADING IN A CRISIS

Leadership is most important under extreme circumstances. Lives, property, and money can be saved or lost as the result of a leader's decision—or failure to decide. Often, however, leaders must decide quickly, with incomplete information, a high degree of uncertainty, and rapidly changing conditions. During crises, successful leaders frequently make use of strict command-and-control structures that employ hierarchical decision-making to ensure responders are all working from the same plan. At the same time, success requires a horizontal network of information-sharing and up-to-the-minute reporting on those crisis responses that are working and those that are not. Relying on experience is important, but so is flexibility—each crisis may be different from the ones before.[21]

While we have not found any universal practices that make effective leadership in a crisis unique from effective leadership in normal circumstances, there are several steps a leader can take immediately during crisis response that will create better outcomes. Chief among these steps is being ready for the crisis to begin with. A crisis management team, engagement with the appropriate external stakeholders, and crisis-response training (including tabletop exercises, scenario planning, and even simulated response exercises) should all be part of a robust crisis preparedness plan.

Once a crisis begins, leaders should establish networks of communication with all stakeholders involved. Next, they should establish a collaborative decision-making process with other organizations responding to the crisis. Third, leaders should coordinate their organization's response with others responding, to match experts from the entire response team to the challenges of the crisis. Finally, leaders should establish a unified command structure to effectively manage the crisis.[22]

Whether operational or symbolic, a leader's behavior matters during a crisis. When an organization or a nation faces dangerous challenges, leaders should maximize their own visibility.

Visibility communicates concern, attention, courage, and control. Leaders should reassure subordinates and all involved in the crisis that they are in command, that there is a plan in place, and that resources have been deployed to overcome the crisis.

Leaders should also communicate constantly during a crisis. Communication is essential to creating effective networks, collaboration, coordination, and successful management. Constant communication can also help to overcome irrational fears and dispel unfounded rumors about nonexistent threats and calamities.

Leaders must act as soon as it is prudent, with a focus on restoring normalcy as quickly as possible. Then, once the immediate threats of the crisis are subdued, leaders should attempt to return to normal, even calm, operations. Finally, leaders should initiate what will often become a long process of restoration, creating prevention protocols against future potential crises. Sharing credit for the successful resolution and leaving a record behind to use in potential future incidents can also be added to the leader's to-do list.[23]

BECOMING A BETTER LEADER

Effective leadership is a career-long process. Organizational knowledge and personal networks are essential to success, so unless you have spent many years in the organization you are now leading, there is always a lot to learn, no matter how much success you've enjoyed elsewhere.

If you are starting a new position, remember that every job has its own novel elements. So, contrary to the typical inclination to make significant changes on day one, we recommend that unless the ship is sinking, you take the time to understand your organization before initiating major changes. Use that time to meet with as many people as possible, both internally and externally. Gather knowledge, opinions, joys, and fears. What is working? What is not? Share your perspective as an outsider, as well, and get feedback on your ideas. Build trust, value honesty and candor, and show that you will maintain confidentiality and consider all points of view. Act quickly if you find consensus on low-hanging fruit.

Once you have learned enough to act, promulgate a limited list of action priorities and put them in the context of a vision for the next two to three years. Manage expectations for immediate success but demand the maximum level of effort, intelligence, collaboration, and integrity. Promise and deliver regular feedback on individual and collective performance. Praise and encourage the positive aspects of the existing organization culture while identifying and demanding collective efforts to overcome the culture's dysfunctional elements.

No matter how long you've been in a position, commit yourself to a never-ending effort to be a better leader. Leadership is a craft that must adapt to the process, people, place, purpose, and times. And in this twenty-first-century brain-based economy, lifelong learning is not a luxury but a necessity. Fortunately, leadership is a set of skills and a set of behaviors; it *can* be learned. Almost all of us can become a leader, and no matter our leadership experience, we can all get better at it.

There are several ways to do this, but first and foremost, you must be self-critical and learn from your mistakes. More than likely, you know better than anyone what you are doing well and where you need help. Where you are not succeeding, try new techniques and assess whether they help you achieve better results. Consider an external comprehensive analysis of yourself and of as many senior, middle, and first-level managers as the organization can afford. Hire a professional coach if you think that will help. Consider enrolling in a professionally oriented graduate program, particularly if you can find one that will allow you to earn a degree while working. Attend programs that provide training in relevant areas that you feel underqualified in. Observe successful leaders, both in your field and in other professions; no doubt you will observe behaviors, skills, practices, and knowledge that you can model, improving your effectiveness.

Learning to be a better leader makes a difference. In our decades of research on management and leadership, we have found that organizations behave differently under different leaders. It makes sense, then, to commit to being leaders that make our organizations, and thus our societies, better for everyone.

3

BUDGET, MANAGEMENT, AND CONTROL

A core responsibility of leaders and managers is to ensure the long-term viability of their organizations. Achieving that objective requires a clear vision of the organization's mission and a strategy to achieve it. And to actualize that strategy, the organization must secure the financial resources to not only find and hire the right people but also to acquire the necessary facilities, equipment, and technology. Once revenues have been generated by the organization's strategy or business plan, those financial resources are then allocated through an annual budget process.

If the annual budget process focuses on revenue generation, it may also be the de facto strategic plan in many organizations. In that case, leaders and managers use the process to gather the information they need to decide how to best allocate the available financial resources to achieve strategic objectives. Simultaneously, management must make sure that the annual flow of revenues is sufficient to cover the planned spending levels. Once the projected revenues and expenditures are decided, the budget implementation process controls spending usually below the budget allocation to ensure that the budget ends the year in balance.

Using the budget process as a strategic plan can work as long as management actually makes budget allocations in line with strategic objectives. If they do, financial resources are then immediately available to address strategic priorities. The annual budget process also assures that the opportunity to address those priorities, or to switch priorities, occurs at regular, annual intervals.

Unfortunately, there are also several major disadvantages when using the budget as a substitute for a separate strategic plan. First, most annual budget decisions are based on the current year's allocation for each activity or program. Next, budget managers look to the previous year's budget before making recommendations for the upcoming budget year. As a result, budget-making is inherently conservative and reactive rather than risk-taking and proactive. In some organizational settings, that method can be functional, but in others it will be dysfunctional.

Making budget decisions annually encourages sound financial management practices and provides frequent opportunities to adjust spending levels based on unexpected changes in the overall fiscal circumstances. As a result, the budget process mitigates against longer-term strategic thinking and discourages managers from fully committing to a multi-year agenda, since they have little or no assurance that adequate funding will be available if the program, product, or activity continues to grow. Innovation is also discouraged when the budget is the same as the strategic plan, as new programs or products have no current or previous budget line. Similarly, less-effective or even outmoded activities continue to be funded much longer than they should be, because they already have a budget line, and incrementalism rules most budget decision-making.

Used properly, however, the budget process is an extremely valuable management tool. In this chapter, we discuss how to use the budget process most effectively—to gather information, to make financial decisions, to control organizational behavior, and to manage financial uncertainty.

GATHERING INFORMATION THROUGH THE BUDGET PROCESS

The budget process is an extremely useful tool for managers to gather information about how products, services, and programs are performing in all levels of the organization. Managers (and even line personnel) are willing, if not eager, to provide information as quickly as possible if they know it will influence their budget allocation in the coming year. Mid-level managers provide senior management with the information they believe will help support the hiring of people, the financing of activities, or the purchasing of equipment and technology. This information, however, requires critical review, since mid-level managers are likely to provide information that is favorable to their request and may discount—or even not disclose—data that is unfavorable or would reflect negatively upon their performance or plans. You can mitigate biased information from those who have a vested interest in its use by requiring the provider to include benchmarks from comparable organizations, competitors, global leaders, as well as independent studies by academics, think tanks, and consultants.

Senior managers can retain consultants to review this information, but this can be expensive. Some organizations have an independent unit devoted to conducting performance measurements and audits of other units. A low- or no-cost alternative is often available from local universities seeking projects for their graduate management students (and other subject-matter experts). These reviews are generally of very high quality, completely independent and objective, and almost always timely, as the students and professors have end-of-semester deadlines.

THE BUDGET PROCESS FORCES CHOICES

A major benefit of the annual budget process is its mandated deadlines and interactivity. Choices must be made among programs, services, and products, and failure to meet deadlines can cut off funds for the entire organization. A widely known example of this dynamic is the all-too-frequent threat by the U.S. president or Congress to shut down the government by refusing to pass the federal budget unless a particular priority is funded at the desired level. In the private sector, decisions to close existing factories or open new ones follow analyses of capital and operating costs and are part of a corporation's normal resource-allocation process.

At the same time, senior managers must be aware of the inherent biases of decisions made based on the budget process. First, the entire budget process is dominated by finance experts who are primarily focused on achieving either a balanced budget (in the public sector) or a return on investment or profit (in the private sector) and who follow sound financial-management practices. They are, at best, agnostic about what is funded and, at worst, biased toward activities that require the least long-term demand for expenditures. Simply put, decision-making based on the budget process is driven by fiscal issues first and mission-related priorities either second or not at all. Financial managers prioritize cost control over organizational outcomes.

Such a decision-making process is also a zero-sum game within organizations. An increase in one part of the organization requires a decrease in another part. In this context, new activities have very little chance of being funded, and activities needing a large increase in staff or a major technology upgrade are at a big disadvantage. For the financial people running the budget process, it really doesn't matter which part of the organization gets more funding as long as others get less in a matching or larger amount. In the long run, this type of decision-making can be catastrophic for the organization. The budget process is biased toward the status quo and gives little or no attention to the mission of the organization. In contrast, effective managers demand that funding levels be based on the degree to which the activities receiving funds contribute to achieving the organization's mission, meeting performance metrics, and/or generating revenues.

THE BUDGET PROCESS CONTROLS ORGANIZATIONAL BEHAVIOR

A budget process enables management to effectively control spending, reallocate resources throughout the fiscal year, mitigate waste and corruption, receive regular reports on revenues and expenditures, and ultimately account for how receivables are spent. Periodic reports (daily, weekly, and quarterly) give managers ongoing information, enabling them to slow down or increase levels of spending or to take money from one activity and give it to another. Managers can rebalance priorities throughout the fiscal year or take across-the-board action in light of current performance, customer demand (or lack of it), or macroeconomic trends.

One particular element that has a significant impact on how the budget influences organizational behavior is the format of the budget document itself. Five common budget formats illustrate how budget structure impacts decision-making: line-item budgets, program budgets, performance budgets, operating budgets, and capital budgets.

Line-item budgets provide a standard format for each unit within the organization. Funds are organized by purpose, typically (1) staff or personnel (often with subcategories of full-time and part-time staff, and sometimes contract staff, temporary help, or seasonal employees), (2) "other than personal service" (OTPS can include supplies, equipment, contracts, technology, transportation, postage, and shipping), (3) fringe benefits, and (4) debt service. In standard practice, a manager is limited by an overall spending limit but is also restricted to spending the suballocations on the line-item category to which they are assigned. That is, they cannot take surplus funds for staff and use it to buy a computer unless—and not until—the central budget director moves those funds from personnel to OTPS. In many systems, they could not even use excess funds allocated to full-time staff to hire a part-time employee without a budget modification.

Thereby, line-item budgets maximize senior management control, fiscal accountability, and tracking. They also limit corruption and waste. At the same time, operations managers are strictly limited, both in discretion and flexibility, to deal with changing circumstances; for example, if funds are locked into a "hiring personnel" line item, managers are unable to save money by instead allocating funds toward technology or contracting, even if those options are more effective and economical.

Program budgets (also called activity, product, or service budgets) replace line-item spending categories with the activities for which the funds are allocated. In this form of budgeting, a lump sum is provided for the specific program, product, or service being produced. Managers have the flexibility to spend on people, equipment, supplies, and contracts in any combination that they believe will best achieve their mission (subject to existing contract provisions, regulations, and labor agreements). Accountability shifts from a focus on spending to a focus on organizational outputs.

Performance budgets use the program budget format and then add measures of organizational performance. As with the program model, managers have the flexibility to spend across budget categories in ways they believe will best achieve their mission, but they now have a clear mandate to meet one or more performance targets, set in advance by senior management after consultation with mid-level activity managers.

Two other budget formats are crucial to understanding how format influences organizational behavior—the operating budget and the capital budget. The *operating budget* funds the organization's activities for the year and includes both expenditures for all activities and a separate table of revenues funding those expenditures, typically for one fiscal year (which may be concurrent with or cut across the calendar year). Expenditures include salaries, OTPS categories, contracts, fringe benefits, and debt service due in that fiscal year. Revenues are also limited to those received within the fiscal year and include such receipts as sales of goods and services, tax revenues, gifts and donations, grants, and user fees. The operating budget provides an overview of the current fiscal health of the organization.

A *capital budget* typically includes funding for large expenditures and projects that take three, five, ten, or more years to complete. Examples of capital expenditures include a bridge, a new building, a supercomputer, a ship, an airplane, a satellite, a new water or sewer system, or a power plant. Funding for such projects is typically financed through the sale of equities, a long-term loan, or the issuance of bonds. When loans or bonds are used to generate capital, the financial obligation is often repaid over a period of twenty years or more. Revenues to repay the debt might include those generated by the capital investment financed, such as sales from a new factory's product line; tolls on bridge, water, or sewer use; or monthly utility bills. The repayment timetable is often matched either to the amount of fees that will likely be generated or to the length of time the asset will be in active use (the period of probable usefulness).

MANAGING FINANCIAL UNCERTAINTY

The annual budget process is inherently conservative and biased toward the status quo, while the environmental context of most organizations is generally dynamic, particularly in terms of macroeconomic factors. Effective managers deal with this divergence using several mechanisms.

One such mechanism is the creation of a pool of unallocated funds, often referred to as an innovation fund or rainy-day fund. This cash reserve makes financial resources available so that managers can take advantage of new opportunities or deal with sudden threats. The unallocated funds are secured by annually eliminating one or more existing activities that are no longer effective or for which there is little customer or stakeholder demand.

In years when financial uncertainty creates expectedly high revenues, this fund is capitalized with all or part of the year-end surplus. The fund can then be used to offset a projected budget deficit in future years. As the rainy-day fund grows, it can also be used to fund capital expenditures that increase efficiency over time—weatherization, computerization, web-based solutions—and then part of the operating savings can be used to recapitalize the fund. Rainy-day funds can also be "borrowed" during the fiscal year to smooth out mismatches between the timing of expenditures and the receipt of revenues, without resorting to external loans that charge fees and interest.

Other longer-term mechanisms to address financial uncertainty include contracting for services from other organizations, outsourcing some activities, creating more effective supply and value chains in the production of goods and services, and forming project-based and more comprehensive partnerships with other organizations, including cross-sector partnerships between and among public-, private-, and social-sector organizations. (We discuss these methodologies in chapters 8 and 9.)

Another way to stay competitive and efficient is merging activity units and consolidating divisions, thereby reducing overhead and streamlining operations. Such actions eliminate the need for personnel, equipment, supplies, and space. Flattening the organization's bureaucratic hierarchy can speed up decision-making while also reducing the number of middle- and lower-level management positions. Coupling position reductions with new gainsharing and performance bonuses for those taking on additional responsibilities can offset any negative impact on morale while better matching compensation with performance.

Another mechanism is investing in new technology, which can not only improve efficiency and outcomes but also reduce operating costs. Technology can be used to increase financial control, generate more detailed and timely financial reports, and ultimately improve the efficacy of financial decisions. Technology can also better connect managers to suppliers, stakeholders, and customers, thereby reducing waste and increasing positive outcomes. Web-based sales and services, artificial intelligence, and robotics all have the potential to improve the quality of goods and services, increase efficiency, and lower costs.

Finally, to offset the impact of unexpected economic downturns, organizations can defer some expenditures by moving them into the next fiscal year. Managers can also offer incentives and discounts to encourage providers of revenue to accelerate payments into the current fiscal year. One-time revenues, such as grants, donations, and asset sales, can also help close a budget gap.

FINANCIAL MANAGEMENT CAN LIMIT ORGANIZATIONAL IMPACT

Financial management and operations management are not identical. Relying on the budget process, financial reporting, and accounting alone can limit an organization's ability to achieve its mission. Too often, financial management is overbalanced toward expenditure control and reduction. In a private-sector organization, ending the year with a surplus of revenues above plan is always good from a financial perspective; from a mission perspective, however, a surplus can actually be viewed as negative. (Note that the nonprofit sector differs in this area. In the private sector, surplus is simply profit and is expected to be as high as possible, but in a nonprofit, a year-end surplus could mean a potential client unnecessarily spent a night in the cold or a child went without food, even though funds were available to provide them with three meals a day.) In a private organization, if senior management is unduly focused on budget balance, they may underfund quarterly investment allocations, thus lowering the organization's ability to achieve its goals. Underfunding normal organizational actions can also create an unmanageable overage of funds in the year's final quarter, encouraging managers to make wasteful spending choices to avoid the impression that they were overfunded. Similarly, across-the-board cuts can create an artificial profit or revenue surge for a quarter or even an entire year. This is not only deceptive but can also weaken the long-term viability of the organization. Due to the seasonal nature of many organizational operations, it is always useful to compare revenues and expenditures to those in the same time period in earlier years.

Overall, the budget process and financial management controls driven by the annual budget process exert a substantial downward pressure on spending. Most managers believe that their unit's work is crucial to the organization's work and, therefore, they are collectively strong advocates for higher spending. Many organizations would rapidly spend themselves into bankruptcy without the fiscal discipline of the comprehensive budget process and its emphasis on a well-understood and well-managed budget. Earnings are taxed in the private sector—as such, accounting systems often report revenues and expenditures in ways that do not match organizational structures. We see other types of mismatches between accounting and organizational structures in the public and nonprofit sectors.

Unfortunately, budget discipline is too often achieved through across-the-board expenditure cuts. This simplistic approach can quickly and easily bring the organization's budget back into balance and even result in a surplus or profit; however, the longer-term consequences of cutting without considering the impact on outputs and outcomes can permanently diminish the organization's capacity to achieve its goals, reduce revenues in excess of the savings produced by the cuts, lower employee morale, and even result in the loss of customers and the best employees.

FOCUS ON REVENUES CAN ADVANCE THE ORGANIZATION'S STRATEGIC GOALS AND FINANCIAL SUCCESS

In many respects, managing the budget is as much a craft as it is a science. But successful leaders and managers recognize that achieving fiscal integrity is essential. Achieving fiscal health solely though the short-term reduction of across-the-board expenditures is perhaps the easiest but least beneficial method of financial control. A combination of targeted expenditure reductions, investments, and revenue increases is a more effective method of fiscal management through the budget process.

In particular, taking actions to increase revenues can be a more effective method than balancing budget to achieve financial success, and it simultaneously helps an organization refocus on its core strategy, enhance its long-term capacity to perform, motivate its employees, excite its customers and clients, raise its profile, and enhance its image and brand. Unlike cutting expenditures, however, raising revenues can require an initial investment of capital and higher spending levels, and it might take time to yield a positive contribution to the organization's financial success. Its success is also somewhat dependent on factors outside the control of senior management, including the macroeconomic climate, actions taken by competitors, and regulatory changes.

HOW TO SUCCEED IN THE BUDGET GAME

Managers seeking to gain additional resources and to avoid expenditure reductions are more likely to succeed if they learn to speak the language of their counterparts in the fiscal division of the organization. Budget managers and accountants focus on current spending levels—the actual results of the most recently completed fiscal year—and make their projections for the upcoming budget based on those numbers. Unit managers must make their case for higher budgets and resist cuts using those same numbers. This might seem very obvious, but in practice, unit managers often seek to dispute the budget numbers from the past and argue for a more optimistic view of the future.

Ultimately, senior management will settle disputes between product, program, and service (or activity) managers and financial analysts. Since the context of the decisions is the budget process, disputing the budget division's numbers is a very high-risk approach. Activity managers are more likely to be successful (and better serve the organization) if they focus on what they know better than the budget managers—how a higher spending level will enable the organization to better serve its customers, retain those customers, attract new customers, create new products and services, become more efficient, achieve the organization's mission and improve the reputation of the organization.

Senior management must assess the merits of each organizational unit's request in the context of both the organization's overall strengths and weaknesses and the current society's opportunities and threats. Senior management must carefully review any proposed "savings" by activity managers, making sure they are not being "gamed" by those managers who are anticipating that either external or internal stakeholders will pressure senior management to restore these savings.

Senior management must also be wary of pilot projects. Such projects may have very modest initial costs; however, if expanded to the full market, a substantial investment of capital and operation costs would be required. Pilot projects can be a fiscally responsible way to test out a new product, service, or method of service delivery; however, senior management must consider medium- and longer-term fiscal demands and potential rewards before funding even the most limited pilot-based expenditure. Experienced budget professionals call this a "nose of the camel" strategy, where a unit manager believes that removing the newly funded service or product from those who have it would result in an intense pressure to provide it to a larger market.[1]

Senior management must also anticipate pressure from external stakeholders, including existing directors, investors, contractors, suppliers, politicians, community leaders, and nonprofit organizations. They must consider whether external stakeholders have been influenced by activity managers seeking to make their case from the outside as well as through the regular budget decision-making process. To a great degree, the politics of the budget process is an internal matter, and senior management should do their best to keep it that way.

The budget process can generate intense organizational conflict, because it most often is a zero-sum game; the budget division must generate a draft budget, which necessarily rejects a significant number of requests from unit managers for higher spending. If the budget division agrees to a new expenditure request from one unit manager, it will generally seek to offset that increase with a cut in spending from another organizational unit. Senior management must ultimately make these tough decisions regarding which managers win and which ones lose. Some of these tough decisions can be avoided if additional revenues can be generated, either as a result of the new spending or from other actions initiated by senior management.

A budget process works best if it gives equal attention to the expenditure and revenue sides of the ledger and considers the connections between actions on expenditures to revenues and vice-versa. There is risk in cutting and increasing both expenditures and revenues. Thus, senior management must make such decisions knowing that the risks also provide an opportunity for the organization to achieve its mission, to grow and enhance its profit, to achieve a return on investment, or to have a positive impact on society.

BUDGET MANAGEMENT IS ESSENTIAL BUT NOT SUFFICIENT FOR SUCCESS

The budget process is a well-established mechanism for setting organizational priorities and making important management decisions. Virtually every senior person in the organization takes the budget process seriously and seeks to participate in it. The process forces senior management to make decisions in a regular and timely fashion, and it enables periodic opportunities to adjust priorities based on changes in anticipated outcomes or the external environment. The budget process builds on lessons from the present and recent past, and its outcomes are easily measured and compared. Perhaps most important, budget decisions on dollars drive organizational results.

At the same time, using the budget process as the primary method for strategic planning and innovation mitigates the ability to abandon outdated and ineffective activities. The budget process looks backward more often than toward the future, and it is focused on the short or, at best, near term. For that reason, the process is not structured to properly evaluate long-term opportunities and threats. The budget process can also exacerbate intraorganizational conflict and destructive competition as part of its zero-sum structure. Overreliance on the budget process by senior management can not only discourage information-sharing, teamwork, collaboration, and participation; it can also focus the organization on cost control over efficiency and productivity.

The budget process and related financial-management tools are extremely important aspects of effective management. To ensure that the organization achieves its mission, the budget process must be directly connected to and driven by a well-developed and widely supported strategic plan (as discussed in chapter 7). And the budget process must be evaluated and subsequently modified by means of an outcome-focused performance management system (as discussed in chapter 5). Budgets should always be subject to mid-course corrections, but these should be undertaken with care because they undermine the certainty and stability of the budget. Commitments of financial resources are the most important decisions management makes, if decisions are frequently reversed, management's credibility is impaired. The way we see it, money is a manager's single most important management tool. Consider this: if you don't pay for something to happen, it will not happen; however, even if you pay for something to take place, there is no guarantee it will happen. Money is an essential—but not a sufficient—condition for organizational behavior.

4

HOW WORK GETS DONE

Human Resource Management, Organization Structure,
and Standard Operating Procedures

Despite increasing automation, when we think about work getting done, we think about *people*. Organizations are collections of people, and motivating people to act and to perform appropriate tasks is the central work of management. We organize people according to specialized expertise and then coordinate the outputs of those specialists into goods and services that generate resources. At the center of management is human resources. More specifically, the job of management is to understand and predict how people and groups are likely to behave.

To start with, people are complicated and difficult to understand, and groups of people are even more so. But in the modern organization, their behaviors have become even more important as more and more tasks are automated. Technology has transformed how work gets done. Work used to require a concentration of people in specific places. Cars were made in Michigan, steel in Pittsburgh, advertising on Madison Avenue, and finance on Wall Street. Now the technology of communication, information, and shipping has dispersed production. This means the people implementing your strategy may be in ten organizations in twenty locations. Face-to-face meetings are still necessary because we are human beings—our species requires them to build trust and make decisions.[1] But many elements of work are communicated by phone, video chat, e-mail, and text messages.

Meanwhile, large, vertically integrated organizations are being replaced by smaller networks of organizations and global supply chains, and the "gig economy"—where more people work independently as contractors for a larger organization—is only growing.[2] This means that some of the people whom a manager must motivate do not work within the manager's organization. In addition, as the service-based economy grows, organizations increasingly run on their brains and their ability to generate creativity, creating an ever-increasing need for managers to understand human resource management.[3]

Complicating matters further, the labor market is changing. It is increasingly diverse, international, and mobile.[4] Unions have weakened, along with individuals' commitments to organizations and organizations' commitments to workers. And in the developed world, people are now looking for more than a paycheck from work; they want a sense of purpose and self-actualization.[5] No matter their organizational home, modern workers typically want a chance to learn and grow and control their own work. They want work that is interesting and that "matters" in some way. They want to stand out as excellent individual performers but also be a valued member of a productive, well-regarded team.

MOTIVATING STAFF

To be effective, motivation must be tailored to the individual. For this reason, a manager must know what makes each person tick. One way to achieve this is to delegate authority; in so doing, a manager can focus on a smaller number of people, discovering what motivates them and how to influence their behavior. A second way is to build working relationships founded on understanding and respect. Successful managers learn to empathize with staff and to discover what matters to them, not only professionally but personally.[6] In operational terms, this means providing flexible work hours and a workplace that respects a worker's personal life. Concern about a worker's family responsibilities, for example, and assistance in meeting those personal responsibilities matters.

In more general terms, motivating workers may involve the purchase of equipment or contracts with vendors to enhance their performance. For instance, an information technology chief may be motivated by the purchase of a new piece of computer hardware or a contract with a cutting-edge cloud-computer firm. Either would be a tangible indication of their value to the organization.

Motivation can also come from the experience of the work itself. The best workers typically report high levels of satisfaction from achievement, recognition, responsibility, advancement, and growth; thus, job *enrichment* is key. This means providing workers with opportunities to take on new responsibilities and to be trained in new skills. It also means encouraging them to speak honestly about work processes, supplies, outputs, and conditions. This is a central tenant of Deming's Total Quality Management, in which workers— not managers—analyze work processes, because they know more about the day-to-day reality of production and customer relations.[7]

In fact, job enrichment is equally, if not more, effective at retaining happy workers than salary. The always important, but often overrated, salary is a necessary, but not sufficient, condition for a motivated workforce.[8]

Finally, in modern complex organizations, a goal of management is to motivate not only individuals but also groups. Very little work is done by one worker alone, so managers must work to build a sense of shared mission and teamwork. This includes articulating the mission and using incentives to reinforce key values, encouraging informal communication and friendships, and monitoring authority relationships to eliminate abuse. In the case of motivating the work of external organizations under contract, an effective manager frequently works with contractor management to structure work and incentives that motivate.

FINDING, HIRING, AND RETAINING PEOPLE

A key aspect of successful human resources management is finding and hiring excellent staff. How do you go about doing that? First, remember that recruitment is regulated by law in all three sectors: in the government sector, it is regulated by civil service law, and in the nonprofit and private sectors, it is governed by affirmative action, civil rights, and employee rights laws.[9]

Beyond that, to find good people, keep in mind these common guidelines:

- Assess your staffing needs.
- Develop a recruitment network of key contacts who can direct you toward talent.
- Use your recruitment and informal networks to encourage good people to apply.
- Develop methods for getting to know prospective workers.

- Use trial consulting or time-limited assignments to identify and recruit talent.
- Conduct a multistage interview to survey colleagues before hiring.

To break down these guidelines a bit more, once you identify potential hires, you must recruit them. Recruiting requires that you learn the rules governing your organization, sell your organization's mission, and frame a compelling offer. It also often requires negotiation, which means flexibility and two-way communication between you and the prospective hire.

Unfortunately, no matter how good your hiring process, it is still possible to make a mistake—in which case, you must learn to manage inadequate staff. Part of that process is to clearly communicate the assessment of poor performance. This should begin informally with a private conversation over a meal or two and, if it persists, be extended to formal performance appraisals.

As part of your assessment, consider that the employee's issues may not be due to incompetence but to an ill fit: put simply, the person and the job may be mismatched. Regardless, if possible, the informal negative assessment should be linked with an effort at outplacement or helping the person find another job. In public environments, where termination is prohibited or extremely difficult, reorganization or an involuntary transfer may be needed to move inadequate performers out of their roles.

In all sectors, however, termination should be the last resort, and it should be used carefully, as its impact on the rest of the organization can be unpredictable. Termination can destroy morale just as much as it can restore it. There are also often legal implications to firing people. Workers in all sectors often have due process and even severance rights under state employment law. And in the private for-profit and nonprofit sectors, the profusion of wrongful-termination lawsuits has made firing increasingly difficult. In some termination cases, for example, former employees have used civil rights laws, designed to provide protection against bias, against their previous employers.

ORGANIZATION STRUCTURE AND DESIGN

Once people are hired, they must be placed within a unit of an organization to ensure that their tasks are coordinated and well managed. An organization's structure details the functions or areas of responsibility assigned to individuals and groups within the organization, along with the reporting relationships between them. Said more simply, structure delineates who does what, who works together, and who works for whom.[10] Reporting relationships and structure are important because they help define an organization's operational priorities. For instance, if a program or production process is decentralized, it may be structured in a way that enables geographic units to dominate functional units. The toxic waste office of the Environmental Protection Agency (EPA) is a good example of this. The regional toxic waste office in New York reports to the head of the New York EPA office, not to the head of the toxic waste office in Washington, DC. This means national policy is more easily influenced by local concerns, and this is by design—to ensure that national policy is mediated by local needs.

Structure also disaggregates work into its component parts and then coordinates those disaggregated tasks to ensure that programs are implemented and that products and services are produced. In addition, structure can be used to reward individuals with promotions, focus attention on a new organizational activity, or address a problem on which stakeholders are demanding action.

An organization's structure facilitates human resources management by achieving the following:

- Establishing a set of work relationships and communication patterns.
- Allowing management to emphasize programs, products, areas of expertise, policies, and tasks.
- Letting people know what they are expected to work on.
- Providing a home for particular standard operating procedures (SOPs) that allows expertise to develop in implementing and revising these SOPs.
- Providing a means to reflect the organization's external environment.
- Focusing interaction and work on tasks related to stakeholders or customers.
- Providing a means to reflect the organization's internal social structure, staff capacity, culture, or history.
- Facilitating internal competition. This is done by giving the same assignment to more than one unit.
- Addressing and resolving conflict and turf issues.

Formal organizational structure is often overrated as a source of management influence. In reality, management influence can grow out of personal history, loyalty, and friendship as much as out of formal authority. And, in fact, informal structure and communication have been shown to be far more durable and persistent than formal structures and reporting relationships.[11] There are benefits to formal structures, however, as much as there are costs. To minimize the costs when deciding upon a formal organizational structure (such as during a reorganization), keep these points in mind: to emphasize one value or function in a structure is to deemphasize another value or function; unanticipated impacts are common; and due to organizational networks, contractor relations must now be carefully considered.

Reorganization is often undertaken in response to new technologies, services, products, programs, or customers. It can be used to emphasize new or modified missions, goals, or objectives. It can also be used to reward excellent performers or punish poor ones. Finally, reorganization can break up dysfunctional patterns of organizational behavior and create more logical combinations of functions to stimulate greater organizational efficiencies. At the start of the global economy, for example, many companies had "international desks" to handle global trade. By the start of the twenty-first century, these units were reorganized out of existence, as all desks became international desks and nearly every major company became fully global.

Reorganization is overused in private and public organizations because it requires few resources and can create a rapid and visible *sense* of change. It can shake up an organization, disrupt old patterns of information flow, and provide management with new information on organizational actions and performance. But reorganization can also hurt—disrupting informal communication patterns, potentially paralyzing an organization, and impairing the implementation of vital standard operating procedures. And though it can be low-cost, it is never cost-free. Leaders and managers who do not fully understand what current organizations do may inadvertently reduce capacity in critical areas of the organization. As a result, reorganization "losers" may leave the organization or, even worse, stay.

The best reorganizations proceed incrementally. They are carried out in small steps, and their impact is assessed before larger steps are implemented. A manager considering a reorganization should engage the organization in discussions about the change. While this might not be possible during a crisis, an effective manager generally avoids sudden, secret, silly efforts to rearrange the organization chart just because they can.[12]

STANDARD OPERATING PROCEDURES

People are hired into organizations to perform particular tasks. While there is always room for creativity and spontaneity in organizations, most work is determined by standard operating procedures. Standard operating procedures are pre-formed, carefully designed actions performed in response to specific external stimuli. When a customer orders a burger at a diner counter, for instance, it sets in motion a specific set of actions in the kitchen. Those actions are standard operating procedures. When an organization's website needs to be updated, the content is developed, approved, designed, and only then placed on the site. This sequence of actions, and their accompanying approvals, are all standard operating procedures.

Standard operating procedures are important because they are linked to an organization's goals and strategies, both of which management is responsible for. Strategy aims to achieve specific, measurable goals and to engage with the organization's environment or market to generate resources. To carry out strategy, managers must develop, complete, and modify standard operating procedures, as needed, to ensure that the organization's work matches the strategy and, thus, to achieve goals.

However, goals and their associated strategies, along with an organization's mission, customers, environments, and technologies, often change. In response to these changes, the design of work must be revised. In other words, standard operating procedures must be revisited regularly and modified if needed. For example, if service requests a switch from toll-free phone calls to on-line forms, the process for responding to those requests must change. Managers can use incentives to encourage the development of new standard operating procedures. Then, once new standard operating procedures are developed, managers may use incentives to train staff to use them. People get used to performing their work in a certain way. If technologies force new SOPs, management may need to provide incentives to staff to change the way they work.

Effectively maintaining standard operating procedures requires leaders to focus on the real work at the heart of the organization. They must ensure that work is both coordinated, to deliver outputs to customers, and divided, or disaggregated, to build separate areas of expertise and their accompanying standard operating procedures. They must also ensure that people who are hired are capable of doing the work, and then they must organize those people into teams within a formal structure. Structure allows staff to focus narrowly on their own standard operating procedures and to develop or purchase the expertise needed to perform those tasks successfully.

CONCLUSION

Despite the changing dynamics of human resource management and its associated areas, organizational structure and standard operating procedures, the fundamentals of work remain. Work requires goals, strategies, task design, hiring, training, and finally the action of work itself. Understanding work, tracking it, and improving it requires a collaboration between staff and management.

As we said in our introduction, management is the art of putting people to work. Now that we've looked at how to motivate people to work, we might say management is also about designing and inspiring people to work. As managers, we must perform this craft within the social system we call an organization—a set of relationships among the people who work in the organization, its contractors, its stakeholders, and its customers—and communication is our key to doing so. When done well, motivating people to work in this way builds identity, loyalty, and the capacity to become an institution: something valued for what it is as well as what it does.

5

HOW WE KNOW WHAT'S BEEN DONE

Organizational Performance
and Information Management

I n the twentieth century, Peter Drucker said you cannot
effectively manage what you do not measure. In the twenty-
first century, the digitization of data, voice, and visual information combined with the low cost of computer capacity to
access, analyze, and draw actionable conclusions has vastly improved the capacity to measure. Today, organizations have
access to a wealth of information on virtually every aspect of
operations, creating the potential for dramatic improvements
in organization management.

More specifically, measurements in the form of big data and
analytics enable organizations to prevent problems rather than
fix them, to anticipate customer demands, and to offer goods
and services before they are asked for. They also allow organizations to tailor outputs to offer place-based or individualized
services.

To harness the potential of measurements such as big data
and analytics, however, organizations need to constantly upgrade their data-gathering, data-analysis, and data-security capacities or contract with a data management firm for these
capacities. Leaders and managers must also determine which

data matters to manage performance and what tools can most effectively hold their members accountable for succeeding.

Taking advantage of today's measurement tools is made even more complicated by our globalized economy. Major advances in communication, transportation, and information make it possible for organizations to locate and operate almost anywhere. Therefore, key elements in deciding where to locate an organization include the quality of governance, public infrastructure, and rule of law in particular areas. Countries and localities must compete for the jobs the private sector provides, and the internet and smart phones further thrust social sector organizations into a global competition for donors. Indeed, our access to information about almost everything going on in the world drives donors and social organizations to at least collaborate. In this global realm, organizations, no matter the sector, must perform at a world-class level if they expect to survive, let alone prosper.

How does senior management go about reaching such a level of performance? There are many ingredients to organizational success—great people, goods and services that customers value, sound finances, a clear mission, and a long-term strategy, to name a few. But how can you identify which workers are great, which goods and services are valued by customers, and whether your finances, mission, and strategy are sound? A robust information and performance management system is essential to ensuring that the organization is moving briskly down the right path.

Building an effective performance management system begins with three foundational steps—benchmarking, defining success, and implementing an accountability system to focus the organization on its progress on the organization's mission.

BENCHMARKING

Here, benchmarking means finding organizations that excel at achieving the components of the mission you want to improve—for example, outputs and outcomes, customer service, efficiency of operations, sustainability, and safety—and identifying their best practices. To benchmark effectively, one should look at industry leaders and innovative startups, as well as organizations from other fields and even other sectors.

Take, for instance, public agencies like the Department of Motor Vehicles that provide driver and vehicle licenses. For many years, these agencies were infamous for incredibly long wait times, byzantine rules and regulations, surly personnel, and outdated technology. Since this service touched a very large portion of the population in many countries, it became a symbol of bad government and the "bumbling bureaucrat." Innovative and mission-driven public servants first succeeded by looking outside their sector at fast-food restaurant chains, banks, and insurance companies to learn how to service large numbers of customers, first in person and later on the internet. They learned to serve customers quickly, efficiently, and courteously without investing large sums in new capital expenditures or recruiting a new and more expensive workforce. Benchmarking is a relatively simple but powerful tool to help an organization zero in on its core mission, the needs of its customers, and the best ways to improve its performance.

DEFINING SUCCESS

As discussed in the chapter on strategy, defining success is a key element of strategy. Defining success is also critically important to improving performance overall, but it is also deceptively difficult. For a private business, success is profit, market share, and return on equity. For the social sector, success is helping people. For government, success is providing its citizens with a safe place to live, work, and enjoy their lives. How true this all is, and yet how incomplete. Depending on the situation, a private organization may prioritize market share, revenue growth, profit per unit, expenditure control, cash reserves, earnings per share, overall debt structure, number of patents secured, or earnings before taxes and debt service. Beyond public safety, governments may also consider the following as indicators of success: the rule of law; due process; air, water, and soil quality; unemployment rate; degree of inequality; average life expectancy; high school graduation rate; debt and the value of currency; and trade surplus or deficit. The social sector may measure how many people helped, how much they were helped, how much it cost to help, how much money they raised, or how many donors and volunteers they have.

Once success is defined, one must then decide which indicators can be used to measure its accomplishment and, further, which aspects of those indicators can be measured. Is the data available to assess changes over time? In each sector, attempts to match success with measurable indicators and the timeliness of reporting can lead to distortions. In the private sector, investors demand data on proxy indicators of success—quarterly revenues, earnings and sales, and projections for the next quarter. This can incent managers to prioritize short-term results over long-term success. In the public sector, governments use trends in standardized test scores for reading and math as the proxy for the effectiveness of elementary and secondary schools. Some governments still use the number of people arrested and jailed as key indicators of public safety, even long after we have learned that crime rates seldom go down as incarceration rates go up. Finally, for many years, a key indicator of sound social sector management was keeping administrative costs below 10 percent of donations. While very high administrative costs may well be an indication of inefficiency or even malfeasance, keeping these costs below 10 percent might actually starve critical functions of resources. In any case, it says nothing about what the other 90 percent is spent on, with the exception of administrative costs.

HOLDING THE ORGANIZATION ACCOUNTABLE

Once management has defined what success is and how it can be measured, they then face the challenge of holding organizations, contractors, partners, and individuals accountable for their performance. This can become a challenge if the performance targets for these people or entities have been set incorrectly. If targets are too much of a stretch, those responsible might not try at all or—even worse—falsify data or cross ethical or legal boundaries to reach it. If targets are too low, those responsible will not reach their full potential or spend the time to improve performance. There is no magic formula, as management remains a craft and not a science. Rather, senior management must track performance closely over time and adjust targets up or down with the support of as much data as possible. To do this, they must constantly ask if the measures being used are truly measuring what is desired. Deming found targets inherently limiting and argued for rigorously measuring current performance and improvement rather than setting targets.

Who should we hold accountable when we miss the target? This requires some thought. Holding one person—or even one division—accountable for sales, or for homeless persons sheltered, or for lives saved in an emergency is generally inaccurate. It can lead to unproductive competition and cause others who might have a material impact to disengage. Holding diverse teams, product line divisions, or geographic locations (precincts, stores, hospitals, or shelters) accountable makes more sense and will likely motivate better performance and higher morale. Senior executives remain accountable for the work of these groups, but they need not mirror individual accountability at every level of the operation, opting where possible for teamwork and group accountability.

Senior executives should also consider that they are not the only audience for performance measures. Customers, citizens, local communities, and the media also use these measures to judge organizations, whether public or private. Engaging these stakeholders in defining and measuring success can benefit business, build political support, and attract customers and donors.[1] And workers themselves often have deep insights regarding how to meet customer expectations, improve productivity, and keep costs down.[2]

Finally, the vast majority of people in an organization will perform in the direction that they are being rewarded and punished. Senior management should be clear with and transparent to employees about which measurable results merit rewards and which ones may trigger penalties. Senior management must continuously monitor performance management metrics to ensure that when performance targets are met and exceeded, employee rewards and recognition follow.[3]

CREATING AND MODIFYING A PORTFOLIO OF METRICS

Peter Drucker is responsible for the seminal work on the art of creating and maintaining an appropriate and effective portfolio of metrics to manage by. He begins by reminding us that what is chosen to measure inherently makes those activities important and will therefore have an overwhelming influence on the results the organization achieves. He also notes that one's choice of metrics should reflect an organization's goals and values—because it will determine them.[4]

What's easiest to measure is *within* the organization and usually includes information on expenditures and revenues. While these metrics can be useful in achieving greater economy and efficiency—thereby improving the "bottom line"— information on results, or organizational outcomes, lies *outside* the organization. Measuring success and failure, therefore, requires *external* measurement. Senior management must develop a system to collect data to measure customer satisfaction, the impact of services and goods, the behavior of those who are not customers, the number of competitors, and the relevant government policies and regulations.[5] A comprehensive portfolio of performance measures must include not only quantitative but also qualitative measures, including ethical, emotional, and psychological impacts connected to the mission and goals of the organization.[6] Within this context, a model portfolio of performance metrics includes four categories of indicators—inputs, work processes, outputs, and outcomes.

Inputs are the resources deployed to carry out the mission, deliver the services, or complete the project. Inputs are measured in time, human resources, assets deployed, and funds committed. Simply put: How hard are we trying to succeed?

Clearly, trying hard is not sufficient, but resources devoted and successes achieved are related.

Work process metrics focus on how well we use the resources allocated to the initiative. How much does it cost to produce a unit of output? What is the cycle time? What is the variation in quality or waiting time? What is the error rate? How much waste is there? How much rework is required? These are the important measures of economy and efficiency. How well is the organization managed?

Outputs are the measurable results of the organization's inputs and process actions. For example, miles of roads paved, meals served, homeless individuals sheltered, patients treated, criminals arrested, smartphones sold, capital raised, accounts opened, or mortgages financed. How much work was accomplished? How much did we produce?

Outcome indicators measure the impact of the outputs. Are we increasing market share, acquiring new customers, satisfying and retaining customers, and increasing profitability? Is the crime rate dropping? Do citizens feel safe? Are high school graduates gainfully employed, attending college, and living happy and productive lives? Is the homeless population decreasing? Are displaced persons returning home? Is life expectancy rising? Is air quality improving and asthma declining? Is our organization changing popular culture and patterns of behavior?

If possible, senior management will construct a performance management system with metrics from all four categories. Sustainable success comes from managing the interactions between the allocation of resources, the efficiency of operations, and the productivity of outputs, and then focusing on the most impactful outcomes. There will be negative interactions between indicators; for example, more stringent safety procedures may cause delays in airplane or train arrivals, whereas emphasizing punctuality at the expense of safety could cause more accidents. Creating the optimal mix of metrics is not easy and will necessarily change over time with use.

The selection of performance metrics and reporting methods is one of the most important decisions made by management. It is a key operational indicator of management's priorities. It can also impact an organization's ability to achieve those priorities. For example, the more metrics you prioritize, the less important each one becomes. On the other hand, what you do not prioritize will be ignored. Reporting data by region, community, or population age or characteristics may provide useful information that enables actions to improve overall outcomes. Alternatively, if those held accountable for a metric also input that data, there is a danger that the data might be manipulated.

There are a few ways to effectively decide on performance metrics and reporting methods. One way is to survey employees on what they think is important and what they believe their performance can influence. Such surveying can build credibility, uncover new opportunities for improvement, and reveal how metrics influence worker behavior and productivity.

Another method is gain-sharing based on metrics, which can reinforce the importance of the activity measured and of performance measurement in general. Gain-sharing based on team performance and larger units of workers can improve morale, communication, and collaboration, while better connecting measurements to the overall mission and broadening measures of success. Shared objectives and incentives lead to more efficient work processes, better problem-solving and cross-training, and a greater sense of shared success.

In the late twentieth century, Robert Kaplan and David Norton developed a methodology called the "balanced scorecard" to integrate strategic planning and performance management. They organized performance metrics into four major categories: financial measures, customer needs/desires/ satisfaction/knowledge, internal business processes (economy and efficiency and measures similar to those involved in Total Quality Management), and learning and growth (learning from workers, empowering them and investing in their education and development—again, reminiscent of Total Quality Management).[7] Kaplan and Norton emphasized the importance of measuring both short-term and long-term objectives, connecting performance measures to key outcomes, and including both quantitative and qualitative indicators.[8] Performance measurement is most effective when its measures not only are drawn from the vision, mission, and objectives set out in a comprehensive strategic plan but also drive resource decisions in the organization's budget process.

THE EVOLUTION OF INFORMATION TECHNOLOGY

At the turn of the twenty-first century, it was not uncommon for a significant percentage of organizational space to be devoted to filing cabinets filled with data—contracts, partnership agreements, bills, copies of checks, medical records, grade sheets, inspection reports, hearing transcripts—the list of categories alone could fill several large filing cabinets. As the decades of this century pass, more and more of our organizations are digitizing old paper records and making new records exclusively digital. We are also digitizing pictures, audio, voice, video, and virtually any type of information that might be related to organizational management. Sensors are more and more ubiquitous, inexpensive, durable, and reliable, and they inhabit most of the equipment and spaces of our organizations and their environments—even our bodies. Our challenge for the future will be deciding which data is most important, how data interacts, and how the available data can improve organizational performance and outcomes. While the amount and quality of data increase exponentially, our ability to process and use information improves modestly, if at all. For decades, a significant percentage of a manager's time was spent gathering and analyzing information to then report to senior management, often with recommendations for improving the organization's performance. Today, collecting data is increasingly automated through the use of sensors, scanners, initial digitization and storage, electronic tagging, and bar codes. The challenge is identifying which information is mission-critical and which information sources are most reliable.

Standard operating procedures should establish protocols for reporting and sharing information, including the frequency of transmission. The goal is to ensure that appropriate and important information is identified and shared rapidly and regularly with the right people in the right places. If possible, important information should be available across multiple platforms—for example, in the office, in the field, on the road, and at home. Security procedures, including encryption, must be robust and continually upgraded since hacking is ever more sophisticated. And in light of security and legal risks, certain information should be relayed only in person. Given these complexities, it is essential that all personnel in the information supply chain receive regular training on proper information management procedures, current threats, and appropriate response and reporting protocols.

Senior management should periodically assess the organization's capacity to access, store, analyze, and report information. Building and maintaining in-house capacity is certainly an option, but this can be costly, and outsourcing can often provide greater expertise and capacity at a lower cost. In either case, the level of security required will help determine what mix of in-house and contracted capacity is the best.

In the twenty-first century, management of information—including communication and associated technologies—is so important and complex that most organizations should develop and operate these activities through a multiyear information management strategy updated at least once every six months. Such a plan should cover these issues: digitization of existing and future data, customer service, worker engagement, transparency, open data and place-based information sharing, and use of sensors and information display mechanisms (including dashboards and other visualization devices). The plan should also include crisis and disaster protocols; rules on sharing across networks (to deal with issues related to access, privacy, ethics, and security); predictive capacity (such as algorithms); personnel recruitment, training, and retention programs; compliance and regulatory capacity; and overall IT governance and accountability.[9] These plans focus senior management on maximizing the effectiveness and efficiency of the organization while also maintaining their values, ethics, and social responsibility.

BIG DATA, ANALYTICS, AND ARTIFICIAL INTELLIGENCE

In recent years, a new world of big data, analytics, and artificial intelligence began to emerge. More and more data became digitized, and existing paper forms and information were converted into digital files. Computing power increased exponentially, costs dropped, and computers got smaller. Today's smartphone has significantly more power than the computers used by NASA to put an astronaut on the moon. As internet and smartphone apps continued to expand, mountains of data (big data) were created in the form of numbers, text, pictures, videos, views, clicks, and sales. More data became available within organizations and for sale from various outside sources. This explosion of data, combined with cheap, fast computers and the emergence of deep learning enabled new possibilities to predict behavior, anticipate emergencies, prevent problems before they occurred, heal and educate others from thousands of miles away, and contribute to the development of self-driving vehicles.[10]

Deep learning consists of algorithms that process massive amounts of data to make a decision or recommendation that is optimized for a specific outcome. Algorithms can help decide which buildings to inspect first to prevent a fire, which drug or behavioral change will most likely prevent a heart attack, or which ad placement will most likely result in a sale. As it progresses, the combination of big data, analytics, and artificial intelligence could take performance management from being a tool to enable better decisions to being a system that makes decisions and achieves desired outcomes.

If fully realized, this advanced system of information and performance management could eliminate millions of jobs currently done by humans, restructure the way organizations operate, and likely redefine work for a large segment of the world's population. We have already begun implementing this revolution.[11] Building data through the many new sources of digital information is already making internet-recommendation engines more and more effective in predicting what each user will want to read, watch, or buy, and placing the relevant advertisement or recommendation in front of them.

Rapidly growing data used to make financial decisions will speed up those decisions, customize terms, and reduce defaults and nonpayments while simultaneously increasing access for customers. The same benefits will accrue in the health care sector, where the speed and accuracy of diagnoses will lower costs, expand access, and improve public health. We can expect similar improvements in elementary and secondary education where data and artificial intelligence (AI) will individualize homework and learning so that each student can focus more on learning what comes less easily while still benefitting from the socialization and team-building of a classroom.

While the benefits of these changes will be profound, we expect the human role in organizational life to continue to evolve. Our expectation is that the craft of management, liberated from some of the drudgery of organizational routine, will become more creative and interactive. In sum, automation, increased and low-cost computational power, and inexpensive instant communications have already made our organizations more productive and innovative, and we believe this trend will continue.

MEASURING SOCIAL IMPACT

Success is how you define it. Traditionally, we would expect social impact measures to be relevant only for social sector organizations and many government agencies, but that is changing. Surveys indicate that young people rank creating social value above profit as the primary purpose of business and say that making a positive difference in the world is more important than professional recognition.[12] And indeed, dealing with many of the most important challenges of the twenty-first century—inequality, education, health care, climate change, hunger, conflict, and human rights—will require contributions from all organizations, regardless of sector.

Therefore, measuring social impact will become a standard component of performance management systems. The metrics that will be used are still evolving, but there are already extensive tools and methodologies for senior managers to consider.[13] Among the most widely known measures are the UN World Health Organization's Disability Adjusted Life Year (DALY), which quantifies the negative impact of poor health and premature death, and programs that reduce these negative statistics are already making a positive social impact.

The Organization for Economic Cooperation and Development (OECD) uses the Social Internal Rate of Return to compare the social costs and benefits of national investments in education, and it has been used to measure the impact of infrastructure investment among other major program investments. Acumen, a large nonprofit organization focused on alleviating poverty, developed the Best Available Charitable Option (BACO) measure, which focuses on the cost effectiveness of various social-impact programs. The Social Progress Index aggregates social and environmental indicators from 128 countries. The Robin Hood Foundation has developed an extensive set of metrics and formulas dedicated to predicting a cost-benefit ratio for various program options to fight poverty.[14] And more recently, Howard Buffett and William Eimicke proposed the Impact Rate of Return (IRR), which enables organizations to project how much impact (which they define) can be achieved for every dollar spent.[15]

But perhaps the most comprehensive effort to establish a standard for social-impact measurement is the Global Impact Investing Network (GIIN), established by the Rockefeller Foundation. GIIN subsequently partnered with J. P. Morgan Chase and the U.S. Agency for International Development (AID) to create the Impact Reporting Investment Standards (IRIS) to provide more than 500 measures of social change. Taken together, all these efforts are moving the science of measuring social impact to a higher level of precision and utility, so that the measurement of social impact will become as indispensable to performance measurement as financial measures are today. These aspects of performance measurement can be expected to develop as a central element of organizational performance management systems, as demand for broader measures of organizational impact develop.

As this chapter indicates, performance management is evolving, and it will continue to increase in importance and use as a management tool. It is a management fundamental that is particularly sensitive to improved technology. Both productivity and customer satisfaction will improve in the future as this tool becomes more sophisticated and integrated into routine organizational work and decision-making.

6

SUSTAINABILITY AND MATERIAL MANAGEMENT

This chapter will define sustainability management, a relatively new and growing element of organizational management. After introducing the overall concept of sustainability, we then discuss the specific steps involved in sustainability management: observation, analysis and delineation of specific actions. Once we know what an organization needs to do to manage itself according to these principles, the question becomes: How do we bring these new tasks into our organization? We briefly outline the steps and alternative means available to integrate sustainability management into routine operations. The chapter concludes with a discussion of the importance of scientific literacy for twenty-first-century managers. In an increasingly complex and technological world, avoiding science and math has become more difficult. Senior managers do not need to be scientists but to be successful they need to understand and motivate people with deep technical expertise.

DEFINING SUSTAINABILITY MANAGEMENT

The field of management has evolved throughout the past hundred years, encompassing changes in mass production and operations research, social psychology, accounting, finance, information management, network management, globalization, and now sustainability. Sustainability management is a relatively new and growing element of organizational management. As the planet's human population and level of material consumption has grown, managers have needed to pay more attention to their organization's use of natural resources and their impact on the natural environment.[1]

The concept of sustainability management has its roots in the field of *sustainable development,* as first defined in the 1987 Commission on Environment and Development, or the Brundtland Commission, as "Development that meets the needs of the present without compromising the ability of future generations to meet their own needs."[2] *Sustainability management* is the organizational management practices that produce sustainable development. It results in economic production and consumption that minimizes environmental impact and maximizes resource conservation and reuse.[3]

Sustainability managers think about the long term instead of focusing only on weekly, quarterly, or daily performance and finances. In our view, effective management is no longer possible without sustainability management, because physical constraints and environmental impacts are increasing their input into organizational decision-making. In addition, maximizing sustainability enables an organization to reduce expenses and maximize efficiency. Part of the rationale for sustainability management is the same as that for Total Quality Management: by driving waste from the production process, managers make the organization more efficient. And lower resource demand means lower production costs.

Another part of the rationale for sustainability management is in a more crowded world, the probability of one organization's production or consumption process damaging another organization's production or consumption process increases. In the words of Paul Simon's famous song; "one man's ceiling is another man's floor."[4]

Sustainability and the practice of becoming more aware of negative externalities obviously make sense, but there are practical obstacles to managing our way to sustainability.[5] Despite these obstacles, the alternative to sustainability management is also problematic. Global communication has made it possible for the poorest of the poor to see images of the developed world on a regular basis. This has resulted in political demands for the developing world to develop.[6] And the only way worldwide global economic development is feasible is if we learn how to manage a high-throughput economy that does not destroy the planet. So, we need to pay careful attention to our impacts and steer production and consumption toward practices that minimize environmental damage.

Some people question whether there is enough capacity to produce the food, energy, water, air, and biological necessities required to sustain human life while maintaining a healthy planet.[7] Our view is that with careful management and technology, there is. It will require sufficient natural resources, technology, and organizational capacity. It will also need to rely on the nearly infinite resource of the sun and its translation to material goods through photosynthesis. We don't have the sustainability technology we need yet, but we will develop it over the next several decades.[8] Managing the planet is beyond our current capacity, but the goal of the field of sustainability management is to develop these capacities.

The capacity needed for sustainability management includes new technologies in the following areas:

- **Water.** We must distribute, process, and used this increasingly rare resource efficiently.
- **Waste.** We must learn to clean sewage and other waste, treating it as a reusable commodity instead of as something disposable.
- **Food**. We must mass-produce this commodity while retaining the capacity for its regrowth and regeneration.
- **Energy.** We must harness renewable energy.

To implement the new technology effectively, we will need the following:

- Specific measurements of the planet's conditions to help us identify problems and the success or failure of new solution-seeking technology.
- Public policy to ensure that sustainable technologies are put into use throughout the world.
- Time to adopt new technologies in addition to incentives for accelerating adoption.
- Capital to develop new technologies.

Incorporating new technologies into human organizations is always a challenge. Likewise, the challenges of adopting new technology to manage sustainability are profound but not intractable. For one, standard operating procedures are persistent and slow to change, so implementing sustainability management practices and technology will require what any organizational innovation requires: incentives to change behavior, resources to pay for incentives, and skill to apply those incentives. It will also require new ways of thinking about resource use and waste. Managers will need to learn how to integrate sustainability factors into routine management and to develop a deeper understanding of integrated human-natural systems.

THE WORK OF MANAGING
ORGANIZATIONS SUSTAINABLY

The first step in the physical dimensions of sustainability at the organizational level is to give someone in the organization responsibility for the work of sustainability management. This can be a consultant; a staff person at a strategic location in the organization; an existing division within the organization, such as the facilities unit; or a newly created sustainability office. Many organizations have opted to develop a new office, in order to communicate the importance of the function and to impress stakeholders and environmentalists.[9]

The next step toward sustainability is to inventory and analyze the organization's use of material resources, such as energy, water, plastics, paper, wood, chemicals, and metals.[10] The analysis should first focus on efficiency and the potential environmental damage caused by material use. Next, the type and amount of materials wasted during production should be inventoried and analyzed. The analysis should address questions such as: Can waste be reduced? Can it be recycled? How is it disposed of, and what is its environmental impact? What is the environmental impact, if any, of the organization's products or outputs? How can it be reduced?

Targets of sustainability management analysis include an organization's facilities along with its transportation of people, supplies, and products. In some service organizations, these target areas may be the only parts of the organization that are inventoried and analyzed. In organizations that use large amounts of information, its data-management facilities or "data farms" may also be a focus of attention. In organizations that outsource services or products or that purchase supplies, the sustainability of the supply chain must also be assessed. Changes in technology; the probability of natural events such as forest fires, droughts, and hurricanes, and other factors external to the organization must also be monitored and understood.

Once an organization's environmental impact is analyzed and understood, the focus of sustainability management turns to developing and implementing practices that reduce those impacts. This process involves applying technologies and standard operating procedures that have been benchmarked from other organizations. It also involves adapting some "off-the-shelf" technologies and practices to the specific conditions of your organization.

When framing sustainability practices, it is critical to both monitor and understand changes in environmental conditions, social and cultural trends, and technological progress. For example, a renewable energy strategy that you once had to dismiss might become feasible when a better and less expensive battery technology hits the market.

The skills required of sustainability managers are the same as those required of general managers: leadership, finance, marketing, regulatory, strategic, and communication skills. But sustainability managers also need to learn to understand the physical dimensions of sustainability and to deploy and comprehend the work of experts in energy, water, waste, ecology, architecture, design, and environmental engineering. This skillset typically requires a more scientific background than many graduates of business, management, and public policy schools have. Finally, sustainability, like many elements of modern organizational management, requires managers to have the ability to coordinate the work of teams comprised of many areas of expertise.

INTEGRATING SUSTAINABILITY MANAGEMENT INTO ROUTINE OPERATIONS

The goal of sustainability management is to eventually be folded into organizational routine. When thinking about sustainability as an organizational function, we find it useful to compare it to an organization's development of information technology or global operations. In the early days of the globally networked supply chain and product marketplace, many organizations had international offices. These groups could help navigate the vagaries of global commerce. By the second decade of the twenty-first century, these "international offices" had largely disappeared as global issues permeated the organizations.

Another major path of innovation at the end of the twentieth century involved information technology, communications, and performance measurement. Many organizations created information offices and appointed chief information officers.[11] Many of these information technology (IT) shops have persisted to keep up with changing technologies, but they, too, no longer have a monopoly on these functions as many specialized organizational units end up developing internal IT and communication capacity.

The ultimate configuration of the sustainability function is less important than the fact that it is performed. An organization may or may not have a chief information officer, a head of global operations, or a sustainability chief, but a well-managed organization needs to operate globally, focus on environmental sustainability, and use appropriate communication and information technologies. The organizational form of this new capacity should follow the function it is required to perform. The purpose of these innovative functions is to enhance the organization's performance—not to show the world how "modern" it is.

SUSTAINABILITY MANAGEMENT AND SCIENTIFIC LITERACY

As management has become more sophisticated, it has become more multidisciplinary. Mass production requires an understanding of statistics, supply chains depend on operations research, accounting depends on economics and finance, and performance measurement requires an understanding of information technology. Different types of production processes require the various disciplines brought together in engineering: mechanical, electrical, hydrological, civil, and environmental. Sustainability requires at least a rudimentary understanding of environmental science and ecology. This is not a field that has traditionally attracted aspiring organizational managers. Fortunately, there is a growing body of literature in very basic and accessible environmental science that can be understood by nonscientists and can help guide efforts to enhance an organization's environmental sustainability.

Rapid changes in technology can disrupt stable and long-standing organizational processes and business models. In every field, managers must monitor technological developments, a task that cannot be undertaken by a scientific illiterate. It is impossible to understand every field of science and technology that might affect your operation. Therefore, the task of today's manager is to learn how to learn new scientific facts and theories. This can range from learning about the feasibility of new energy and production technologies to understanding the environmental impact of an organization's waste stream. Just as in many other areas where general managers depend on the work of skilled experts, managers must have conceptual frameworks they apply to answer key questions such as: How does this work? How certain are we? What does this cost, and will the cost change over time? Can it be scaled? How will this impact current operations? How will this impact stakeholders and customers? And then the key sustainability question: How does this impact our planet's ecosystems?

CONCLUSION

Sustainability management has its roots in environmentalism, so it is sometimes dismissed by "hardheaded" managers who see it as soft public relations and unrelated to the important work of organizational management. Our view is that sustainability management owes it origin in management theory more to J. Edwards Deming than to Rachel Carson: Pollution is waste; inefficiency is waste. Sustainability management is about saving energy, water, and other raw materials. It is about finding a use for material substances in production instead of dumping it into the river. It is like how your grandmother managed a chicken: every part is used and nothing is thrown away.

On a crowded planet of growing economic consumption, these principles are necessities and not luxuries. If your competitor is using these principles and you are not, you will lose out on price. If another city is governed according to these principles and you are not, that other city will attract people and businesses, and you will not. In other words, your organization cannot afford *not* to adopt sustainability management.

PART II
THE ORGANIZATION AND ITS ENVIRONMENT

7

STRATEGIC PLANNING

Organizations need goals and a plan for achieving those goals. Thus, an organization's strategy identifies two fundamental elements: (1) the organization's short- and long-term objectives and (2) the methods and actions that will enable them to achieve those objectives. A real strategy also delineates the resources to be used to pay for the planned actions; a strategy without resources is only a symbolic exercise of limited use. As we will see, all strategies involve decisions about what the organization should and should not do.[1] And all are constrained by competitive, political, social, and economic factors.

THE ELEMENTS OF A STRATEGY

Every strategy should be built on an explicit or implicit strategic plan. There are six basic elements to any strategic plan:

- Problem and opportunity analysis
- Identification and analysis of parties or stakeholders
- Historical analysis

- Organizational and situational analysis
- Identification of key organizational goals and actions
- Assessment of the strategy's probable impact

The *problem and opportunity analysis* is often part of an analysis identifying the organization's strengths, weaknesses, opportunities, and threats (a SWOT analysis). The goal of this analysis is to analyze and understand the factors that impact an organization's ability to obtain resources.[2] We prefer the term "problems" to "threats," since some of these challenges are not important enough to be threats. The questions that must be addressed in this part of a strategic plan include the following:

- What programs, products, and services should we be producing?
- Why do we exist, and how are we unique?
- Who are our customers/users/clients?
- What do we do best now, and what will we do best in the future?
- What are our major outputs and outcomes, and how can we measure them?
- What is the source of our challenges and opportunities?

Identification and analysis of parties or stakeholders is the part of the strategy formulation process that asks the question, "Who?" Who is creating the problems, challenges, and opportunities for our organization? Who are the internal and external stakeholders, and what are their perspectives? How will the views of these parties influence the organization's mission or ability to implement the strategy? How flexible or entrenched are their views? What might induce change? What might generate support or defuse opposition?

The analysis of stakeholders involves an effort to assess the influence and power of these parties.[3] In what way can they influence your organization's ability to generate resources? Are there ways to reinforce their support or deflect their opposition? Often, these questions lead an organization to develop alliances or partnerships or to merge organizations, at which point political analysis is required.

The historical analysis is undertaken because, if we are to know where we are going, we need to know where we have been. How did the problems and opportunities facing the organization evolve? How have different levels and individuals within our organization responded to key challenges and opportunities in the past? Which strategies have worked and which have failed? What is the history of relations with stakeholders? This part of a strategy often requires discussions with past or long-time employees. It can be conceived of as a case study of the organization's history. The goal is to learn from the past and develop a deep appreciation of the organization's distinctive competence.

History is important because, over time, organizations develop myths about themselves, which need to be understood and sometimes discarded. Sometimes the reason "we've always done things that way" is that we didn't know any better. And sometimes we really did things differently but forgot. Examining the past is important for developing a clear-eyed perspective on the present.

The *organizational and situational analysis* is an effort to assess the organization's capabilities and how those capabilities match the expectations of customers and the sources of capital and revenues.[4] How does the organization need to evolve to continue to survive, grow, and thrive? Technologies, culture, and new economic, political, and social realities typically change the demands an organization must meet. An organization must be sensitive to those changes and modify its outputs and production processes in response. A strategy is an effort to anticipate or respond to those changes to keep the organization functioning.

An important part of this analysis is to determine the specific capacities that need to be developed to address new conditions. This might include selling an organizational unit or ending it, forging new partnerships or contract relationships, or hiring or training staff. This can be a difficult analysis to undertake because it can require brutal self-analysis. But the more realistic this self-assessment is, the more useful it will be.

Once the analysis of the organization's internal capacity, stakeholders, and environment are complete, it is time to *identify the organization's key goals and the actions needed to achieve those goals.* Since most resource allocations are planned in annual increments, we have found that strategies should include one- and five-year goals, actions, and resource allocations. The resource allocations are critical, because if a strategy is to be operational, or real, it must be closely connected to a budget process.[5] If the goals and actions are beyond the capacity of the current organization, then either the strategy or the organization must change.

Our view is that the one-year time horizon is more important than the five-year one, because no one budgets five years in advance. However, the five-year horizon is needed to ensure the organization attempts to undertake activities that will take longer than one year to develop. An overly short time horizon will limit the organization's ability to meet future needs.

In addition to connecting strategy to the allocation of resources, managers must connect its progress to the organization's performance measurement system (see chapter 5). A critical element of strategic planning and analysis is assessing the strategy's impact. For this assessment, a manager needs to know if the organization's goals are still relevant and if the organization's actions are producing the outputs that result in the desired outcomes. If the strategy or business model is not working well, the organization may need to make a mid-course correction. It may be that projections of the organization's environment were off and the organization's goals, activities, and resource allocations must change. An honest assessment of performance may lead to an effort to change an organization's culture and its capacity to meet changing demands.[6]

FORMULATING AND IMPLEMENTING A STRATEGY

Once you have decided to develop a strategy, you need to decide on an approach to formulate it. You could hire an outside expert to study and understand your organization and then develop a private plan for your personal review. At the other end of the continuum, you could create an organization-wide or even public effort to undertake the analysis, and brainstorm the steps required to implement a strategy.[7] There is no right or wrong way: strategy formulation is simply a function of the organization's health and the resources that exist for a rigorous self-examination. In some cases, the process can be used as part of an effort to change organizational culture. In other cases, the change required is so radical, a secret process is your only option. Our experience is that organizations in crisis tend to develop strategies in secrecy. It is difficult to know in the abstract if a public process is better than a private one, but again, our experience is that private organizational discussions rarely remain private.

In all cases, serious strategy formulation costs time and money. Someone important in the organization must manage it, and access to organizational decision-makers is a prerequisite to a meaningful process. Many people have experienced strategic-planning processes that were symbolic, "window-dressing" exercises without meaning. A more substantial process requires meaningful efforts to develop consensus among (at a minimum) powerful stakeholders.

Once a plan is in place, the trick is to bring it into daily organizational life and to make it a living, breathing process that sets direction but is constantly revised. Strategic objectives and actions need to be translated into normal organizational responsibilities and work. To do so, you must use the management or organization structure and the performance measurement system to assign and track strategic tasks. The plan itself must also be constantly changed to match internal and external realities, but the changes must be careful, or the plan itself will lose credibility. Finally, the incentives used to influence staff and contractor behavior must be modified to reinforce the organization's strategy. The strategy becomes a tool for communicating management priorities and direction, and the organization justifies its allocation of resources to enhance its implementation.[8]

THE NEED FOR STRATEGY

The principle reason that organizations need a strategy or business plan is to attract resources. If an organization doesn't produce anything that is valued by customers, clients, or those who control resources, it will die.

By requiring a clear sense of mission, a strategy allows an organization to evolve in response to changed conditions and to defend its distinctive competence. It also helps ensure that the organization doesn't take on missions in conflict—because without a clear sense of mission and strategy, an organization is open to being taken over or becoming the repository of another organization's strategy.[9] That type of dependency can limit its freedom of movement and, at some point, threaten its survival.

In addition, strategy is needed to provide a mechanism by which to make choices. You can't do everything, and so you must place your organizational bets in the direction that will use the fewest resources to generate the most resources. Resources are always finite, so to be successful, an organization must focus its efforts in ways that generate new resources. A clear strategic focus has the benefit of defining an organization's shared mission, and if the strategy is public, it can be a method for communicating the mission to the entire organization. A strategy provides an opportunity for the organization to think and reflect on its ends and means. It can provide a process for making trade-offs.

A meaningful strategy is a critical management tool, but it is not without drawbacks. For example, strategies are not cost-free: by deciding what an organization will do, you must explicitly state what it will not do. This can stimulate opposition and impair morale. It can also create the expectation of a massive, non-incremental organizational change, when that degree of change is infeasible. In addition, developing and implementing a strategy can cost a great deal of not only money but staff time, which means staff who do not agree with the strategy may subvert it or leave the organization and possibly join a competitor.

THE PUSH AGAINST STRATEGY

A strategic plan provides a thoughtful, structured way to bring about organizational change. But many people resist change; they believe the adage that "if it ain't broke, why fix it?"

Some seek to be nimble and fast-paced and, for that reason, resist the time it will take to develop strategy. For others, schedules, structure, and rules can be seen as mechanisms that inhibit creativity and innovation. In any case, resistance to change should always be expected. Sometimes the resistance is not overt but passive-aggressive. For example, some people, when asked to join the strategic-planning process or to implement its results, may simply dig in their heels and continue to work as they always have.

But though the costs of strategic planning and explicit organizational thinking should be understood, they typically are worth overcoming. In other words, managers should understand that every organization has interest groups or willful individuals who resist change in order to maintain their power or perquisites, but they should also realize that if a strategy is matched by resource allocations, resistance can be overcome.[10]

CONCLUSION

It is not unusual to see organizations undergo symbolic strategic-planning exercises, but we have never seen a well-managed organization without a clear strategy that was well understood by both its members and by critical stakeholders. Like all tools of management, however, strategy is far more effective when combined with other tools. In particular, combining strategy with the tools of budgeting and performance measurement are essential: strategy and resources must be paired, and performance measures are needed to see if the strategy is working and, if not, how it might be modified.

8

CONTRACTS, OUTSOURCING, SUPPLY CHAINS, AND THE MAKE-OR-BUY DECISION

To succeed in a competitive global economy, all managers must continually address the "make-or-buy" decision: Do we make this ourselves, or do we buy it from another organization? The make-or-buy decision defines an organization's identity: it determines what the organization is and isn't going to be, and it focuses on the organization's distinctive competence. If you start to buy something you once made, you gain the ability to specialize, but you may lose the essence of what made you special. If the decision is made incorrectly, it can lead to the organization's demise.

THE CORE ELEMENTS OF CONTRACT MANAGEMENT

The decision to buy is contracting. Contracting should not be a way of offloading work, but a path to take on work that might be beyond the purview of your organization to enhance the quality of the outputs produced by your organization. In our world of supply chains and organizational networks, much of the work you already manage is likely conducted outside your organization. Contracting can enable an organization to accomplish more goals, more effectively; to design place-based solutions using local organizations; and even to innovate its work processes and information management systems. But you are still accountable for work that is not under your direct control. Therefore, effective managers seek to understand the obstacles to contracting and learn the tools and techniques to use to be successful at contract and vendor management.

To start with, managing contracts consists of several central functions:

- Finding out what contractors are doing and producing.
- Implementing systems of contractor incentives, to ensure contractors do what you want them to do.
- Using incentives and performance tracking to help understand and manage a contractor's work.
- Getting a fair price for services.

A contract can include legal provisions that require performance reporting and even third-party verification of information you receive from contractors, but such a requirement must be included in a written contract agreement, and the information you receive will not be free. One way of reducing your information needs is to use a performance-based contract, where fees are tied to specific deliverables.[1] Then you can manage against performance and pay less attention to the production process. The definition of the deliverable and a process for approving it as acceptable for payment then becomes a central issue in the contract negotiations. It is also possible to structure rewards and punishments in a contract, stating, for example, that on-time or early delivery will be rewarded with a bonus and that late delivery will be punished with a delay or withholding of a portion of the payment.

A key issue in contract management is how involved you should get in the operations of your vendor. Since you decided to buy rather than make the good or service, a rule of thumb is to limit your involvement as much as possible. Nevertheless, you may need to be more involved at the start of a contracted relationship and then taper off as time and experience builds mutual confidence.[2] And it is important to avoid assuming the contractor will automatically deliver whatever you need. Understanding the details of a contractor's work can also help lead to a more realistic price for deliverables.

To manage contracts and contractors, a manager must know or have access to expertise about the laws, regulations, and internal organizational policies governing contracting.[3] Many organizations have rules to prevent conflicts of interest, corruption, nepotism, and self-dealing.[4] In some organizations, there are no internal rules, but there may be federal, state, or local laws that must be understood. When you are contracting with a vendor located in another country, a range of complexities may come into play related to trade law, currency exchange, and local labor laws. The idea that a free market, unfettered by regulation, exists somewhere is a fantasy. Most organizational activity is subject to some form of law or regulation. Nevertheless, the drive toward global networks is so intense that the price of adhering to the law during these transactions is assumed, included in pricing and still incurred by organizations in order to operate globally. In other words, the organizations that participate in the global economy do not assume there is a free market, but even with the cost of regulation factored in, they still find it advantageous to operate globally.

In addition to understanding the rules of the game, a manager of contracted work must understand the vendor's production process and the goods and services it provides. After all, it is difficult to purchase or manage something you don't understand. In general, regardless of the vendor, assuming that a contracted product or service can be turnkey, or provided in completed form, is dangerous and will leave you open to inadequate supplies or overpayment for goods and services.[5] As far as the specifics of deliverables, however, if you don't know what you are buying, gain access to expertise—whether an employee or a third party—that can assist you.

It is also important to understand the culture, motivation, and track record of the organizations you contract with. A contractor should be the subject of the same due diligence you would give a partner. In sum, contract management is like all other types of organizational management. It requires strategy, performance measurement, incentives, and all of the work involved in managing internal staff.

OBSTACLES TO CONTRACTING AND HOW TO OVERCOME THEM

Contracting problems often start when you are not sure what you are trying to buy. In those cases, your requests for proposals and other methods of either eliciting bids or identifying vendors can land you a contract with the wrong vendor. One way to address this problem is via informal discussions with the prospective vendor, where you summarize your needs and determine whether the organization has the capacity to meet them. Another method is to contract with an organization that can either help you discover what you need or assist you in developing a new service or product to use in lieu of a vendor. When the military needs a new weapons system, they will sometimes contract with a company to do the research required to develop a prototype.[6] In other instances, a short-term contract can be let to enable a pilot test or some other experiment needed to develop new capacities.

Another problem can be your organization's rules and procedures for purchasing goods or services. Procurement processes can be so cumbersome that sometimes organizations decide to make something in house simply to avoid the process of buying it. The obvious answer in this instance is to develop a more flexible, streamlined process of contracting.[7] The goal is to ensure that purchasing is encouraged when it is in the organization's interest.

On occasion, we find that there are too few bidders or there is too little competition among the organizations producing the product or service you are hoping to buy. Sometimes, you are looking for something that does not exist, or the available supply cannot meet the demand. In this type of scenario, your choices are to meet your needs in house or to convince an outside organization to develop the capacity or product you need.

Once you have a contract in place, a new set of problems can develop. Sometimes there is poor communication between the buyer and vendor. For this reason, it is often useful to include contract provisions that require communication processes tied to deliverable schedules. For large and important contracts, it is helpful to develop a working relationship between staff in both organizations. Frequent calls, emails, and meetings should be encouraged, and while communication can be formal, most should be informal. Clear milestones and performance measures can facilitate communication, along with inducements to provide bad news along with good news. Sometimes the communication problems originate with the purchasing organization forgetting to provide adequate direction. For example, competitive forces in the purchasing organization can result in conflicting objectives, and as a result, a contractor may find themselves in the middle of a turf war. In those cases, the contractor must seek clarity from the purchaser or risk being penalized for not fulfilling the terms of the contract.

In some cases, what appears as poor contractor performance is actually a reflection of poor management in the purchasing organization. In other cases, the poor performance is due to contractor incompetence. Some firms are great at marketing and business development because they put their most talented people in sales, but they are better at winning work than doing work. It's like the job candidate who gives a great interview but is better at presentation than working. To guard against this potential problem, use contract mechanisms such as specific milestones, frequent reviews, penalty clauses, and even the right to reject some contractor staff from working on your projects.

We addressed performance measurement and management in chapter 5. A poor performance measurement system can make effective contract management difficult if it does not collect data and measure critical elements of the contracted work. Even if the measures are good, the system may have inadequate data analysis, or reporting protocols. Or staff may just not be motivated to maintain the system. To guard against this problem, specify the elements of the performance management system and your role as the client in the written contract. Tie contractor payments to specific measures and reports. And, if possible, require independent auditing of key performance measures. Provisions can require regular reporting prior to periodic invoices and payments, permit the purchaser to require reports in response to performance problems, or do both.

Another obstacle to contracting can develop when a community or a union come to believe that "outsourcing" is another name for "downsizing" or "layoffs."[8] That perception can result in political opposition to contracting, which can be especially difficult to overcome if employment levels are not growing. Outsourcing, automation, and a variety of technological and social changes threaten job security, and organizations must be sensitive to the real fear that these changes can bring.

A well-managed organization in a changing environment needs to make a real effort to work with staff on training, transfers, or other steps that can help them adjust and feel more secure during times of change. Managers need to provide assurances to staff on continued employment and take the steps needed to ensure that staff are prepared for new tasks. Once management has a track record of retaining rather than discarding people, some of the resistance to change should be reduced.

Global competition has established highly efficient supply chains that require modern organizations to constantly change their work processes and their decisions about what to make and what to buy. But the organization's people and their loyalty to the institution is an invaluable asset that must be nurtured.[9] A better supply purchased from a vendor will make a service or product better, but so will a staff with high morale. In our brain-based economy, people matter more than ever. A short-term investment in training or family assistance can pay off in enhanced loyalty and productivity.

WHEN YOU SHOULD MAKE INSTEAD OF BUY: WHEN CONTRACTING IS A BAD IDEA

Deciding what kind of work to keep in house requires an organization to define itself and to determine the irreducible core of its being. This is, again, that concept of distinctive competence: What do we do that no one else does that is key to attracting resources? For example, we work at Columbia University, one of the world's great research universities. While the university contracts with Barnes & Noble to run our bookstore, we would never contract out teaching or research. Those two functions define the university and are the main sources of the institution's revenue.

Organizations evolve and their distinctive competence evolves with them—a service, function, or product that was once central to the organization may become less important over time. For example, IBM once dominated the personal computer market, but in 2005, it sold that business to a Chinese company called Lenovo. IBM was no longer making enough money making PCs and wanted to focus on more profitable consulting services and information networks.[10] But a decision to drop a major product is unusual and difficult for most organizations. IBM made the strategic decision to shed the PC business.

An organization should not purchase a service, good, or function if doing so would impair the organization's capacity and distinctive competence. It is also dangerous to contract for capacity when it does not yet exist, unless, as noted earlier, the contract is to develop the capacity, which would then be "owned" by the purchasing organization. If one attempts to contract for something that does not exist, the odds are that you will not receive bids that allow you to purchase whatever you are seeking.

When deciding to outsource, we suggest addressing (at a minimum) the following questions:

- How central is the function to the organization?
- How much new capital is required to perform this function?
- How much existing capital was invested?

- How much capacity do we have to perform this function, and what are the risks of involving other organizations in the work?
- Is the capacity to perform this function common or rare?
- Does the capacity to perform this function need to be developed and, if so, would it be better for us to have another organization do this?
- Can someone else do this better and cheaper, and are they willing to sell it to us at a good price?
- Does the contractor have a monopoly, and does contracting with them leave us vulnerable in any way?
- Is reliable and punctual delivery assured?
- Are there political, marketing, or other external relations reasons to do this ourselves?

The central issue is the definition and importance of an organization's distinctive competence. The leader's role is to develop and protect the organization's distinctive competence—or its niche or mission. The concept of leadership developed by Chester Barnard in *The Functions of the Executive* and by Phillip Selznick in *Leadership in Administration* focuses on two key aspects of a leader's role. According to them, a leader does the following:[11]

- Looks "up" into the organization's environment to obtain the resources needed to "feed" the organization and develop its distinctive competence.
- Looks "down" into the organization to provide and distribute the incentives needed to develop capacity.

These capacities are those that an organization *uniquely* possesses: what an organization does that enables it to obtain resources from its environment. Here, again, we emphasize the importance of resources. Without resources, an organization dies. An organization's distinctive competence is how it attracts resources. Distinctive competence defines the organization—what is central to it and what is not. If you contract out a core function, you can endanger the organization's survival. In addition, if you make the decision to contract out an organizational function, the capacity to manage outsourced functions must still be retained.

While shedding a product such as a personal computer redefined IBM's distinctive competence, organizations tend to retain functions when they contract. These contracted functions are managed differently than functions produced internally, but they are still managed. A contract relationship changes the management challenges, but it does not change the organization's accountability for the contracted function; management must still answer to the organization's governing structure, which can include elected officials, the public, shareholders, boards of directors, trustees, or a mix of entities.

This accountability to the governing structure is always present in all organizations. Contracting does not change the demand for management accountability. For this reason, management must assure that they have information on contractor performance and the means to influence that performance. The ability to enforce accountability is central to effective contract management. In sum, contracting changes the nature of management influence and control, but it does not reduce its necessity.

All accountability issues are not equally important. Government entities and nonprofits often face life-or-death situations, where the margin of error is smaller. Issues such as foster care, health, war, and criminal justice all have contracted elements, but outsourcing when lives or freedom are at stake must be done with greater-than-usual care. However, even private firms experience potentially dangerous issues of accountability. In a more complex and technical environment, and under conditions of asymmetrical information, it is more difficult to assure accountability by contractors. For example, an airplane may have crucial pieces of software designed by a vendor, but the manufacturer remains liable for any death or destruction resulting from failed control systems.

THE FUTURE OF CONTRACTING

Organizational networks and sophisticated, resilient supply chains are already part of most organizations, and their growth in coming years is easy to project. Obstacles to contracting and extending supply chains can and will be overcome. These changes will lead to an increased demand for contract management skills. The subject of this chapter is not typical in many management courses, and there is very little research on managing contractors.

We think this will change. We expect to see an extension of performance management systems from contracting organizations to their vendors. Ultimately, skill and experience at managing contractors will likely become part of a manager's "toolkit" and join basic skills in accounting, finance, sustainability, human resources, marketing, and information management as routine but essential elements of competent management.

9

CROSS-SECTOR PARTNERSHIPS

How the Three Sectors Differ and
Why Collaboration Is Beneficial

M ost nations in the twenty-first century have their
organizations divided into three sectors—public (government), private (for-profit companies), and social
(nonprofit or charitable organizations). The precise legal classification of a given organization will vary over time and
geography.

In general, however, the purpose and responsibilities of
organizations in each sector leads to a particular focus. The
public sector—government—has the power to tax, take private
property, use force, make laws and regulations, and lay claim
to representing public interest. The private sector is focused on
making money for its shareholders or owners. Therefore, successful private-sector organizations are driven to achieve the
greatest level of economic efficiency in their management,
focused on innovation to attract new customers and gain
market shares, and able to attract—and keep—high-quality
employees, managers, and leaders by providing the highest salaries and benefits that they can afford. The social sector is mission-driven and focused on helping people, other living creatures,
and the planet itself to be sustainable and better for all,
now and in the future. Therefore, social sector organizations

generally place positive outcomes for those they serve above all else. The social sector attracts talented professionals, volunteers, and charitable contributions because of their noble mission and concern with outcomes.

One sector is no better than the other. Each has their particular strengths and weaknesses. From an overall management perspective, many common practices comprise effective management regardless of sector, with differences relating mainly to the core mission of individual organizations; however, the constraints and capacities in each sector are different. That said, there are a number of specific reasons why senior managers of organizations from one sector might partner with an organization from the same or another sector. While contracts between organizations date back many hundreds of years, a more collaborative approach, called cross-sector partnerships, began to take shape in the twentieth century—commonly led by government—and rapidly expanded in use throughout the twenty-first century.[1] We find the Venn diagram in figure 9.1 useful for thinking about how societies are managed and believe it outlines why there is great potential for accomplishing important work through cross-sector partnerships.

At their best, cross-sector partnerships can draw on the best of each sector and avoid at least some of each sector's inherent limitations. Partnerships deliver services, collect and analyze data, raise and deploy financial resources, create and manage capital plans, and supervise disaster preparedness and emergency response among other activities. Some of the major reasons why organizations form partnerships for these activities are to help more people, to make more money, to accomplish what would otherwise be difficult to achieve, to be more efficient, to access new skills and supplies, to create a very special-

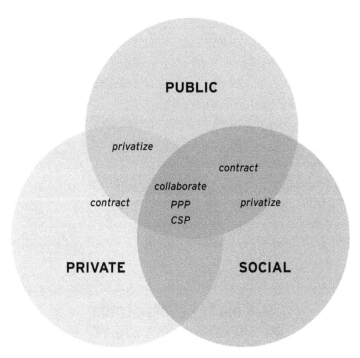

Figure 9.1

ized value chain, to globalize quickly, to reach new customers, and to share risks and costs.

More broadly, the increasing complexity and interconnected global economy in the twenty-first century presents challenges and opportunities that cross national and traditional-sector boundaries. As a result, cross-sector partnerships have formed and succeeded in countries all over the world. They have been used to overcome challenges and achieve much higher levels of performance in a wide variety of areas, including the following:

- Providing water and handling wastewater.
- Building and managing mass transit systems.

- Providing energy.
- Building large public arenas.
- Revitalizing deteriorated urban areas.
- Creating or rehabilitating public spaces for recreation, education, art, and public health.
- Improving the quality and efficiency of public services.
- Providing secure personal identification and access to public and private services.
- Creating innovative telemedicine and internet-based mass education systems.
- Providing more effective rehabilitation and reintegration of people who have been incarcerated.

HOW DID THE CROSS-SECTOR PARTNERSHIP MODEL EVOLVE?

Modern cross-sector partnerships evolved from the government-led public-private initiatives that occurred during the Great Depression and Second World War era. Faced with challenges beyond the capacity of any one sector, the New Deal of President Franklin Delano Roosevelt incentivized (and sometimes mandated) that private companies work with the government to provide jobs to the unemployed; guarantee retirement income; modernize farming; electrify rural areas; build huge dams to generate low-cost power; provide low-interest, long-term loans to increase homeownership; supply the Allied Forces with tanks, planes, ships, and other equipment and supplies; and even expand public arts projects.[2] Government had certainly facilitated private efforts for public benefit—the provision of public lands for private development enabled the private construction of a transcontinental railroad system, resulting in the construction of the national telegraph, and then the telephone network, and then the national electric grid. The difference in twentieth-century initiatives is that organizations from the public and private sectors worked more closely together on the design and implementation of the activity.

After the Second World War, governments around the world took over what had previously been private activities, including mass transportation; automobile, ship, and airplane construction; port development and operation; health care; telephone and electric service; and even radio and television broadcasting and programming. In the United States, most of these activities remained in the private sector. However, the federal government initiated three major programs that partnered government with private companies, which served the public interest and were also profitable for the private "partners."

The National Interstate and Defense Highway Act of 1956 was originally financed by the federal and state government, but it was planned at the state and local levels and was built primarily by private companies, which resulted in the mass investment of private funds in economic development, housing, and infrastructure for decades to come.[3] In the 1960s, the U.S. government's decision to develop a space exploration program under a new agency, the National Aeronautics and Space Agency (NASA), sparked the creation of numerous partnerships among NASA and private companies, to build the infrastructure to send vehicles and people to and from space safely. Like those in the highway program, these partnerships spurred other private investments and inventions that made money and served the public interest—from Teflon and Velcro, to cell phones, satellite television, and microwaves, to name a few. Also, in the 1960s, government programs to provide health insurance for the poor and the aged partnered with private doctors and hospitals to accept government-funded insurance and provide health services.

The modern public-private partnerships were built upon this foundation. Beginning in the 1980s and continuing well into the twenty-first century, public and private organizations came together and operated by means of a formal contract agreement to carry out a mutually beneficial activity or project. Known widely as PPPs, or P3s, these partnerships have built and sometimes operated bridges, desalination plants, roads, stadia, subways, pipelines, and virtually every other kind of infrastructure you can imagine, including the still amazing Eurotunnel. Cross-sector partnerships (CSPs) take PPPs one step further by including social sector organizations as potential partners; further, CSPs generally focus on extremely complicated projects and the delivery of goods and services that serve the public interest.

DEFINING AND STRUCTURING CROSS-SECTOR PARTNERSHIPS

A partnership emerges when managers from one organization identify an important goal, product, service, or project to pursue but they either cannot do it alone or believe that joining with an organization from another sector can help them do it better. As we discussed in chapter 8, organizations work with other organizations all the time, through contracts, outsourcing, and value chains. There is a long history of private firms working together through supply chains, mergers and acquisitions, and joint ventures. In the public sector, intergovernmental agreements are plentiful as well. In both cases, there is a complex legal and regulatory structure that has developed. But these collaborations are different from CSPs because they occur *within* sectors (private/private, government/government, and social/social) rather than *between* them. In comparison, CSPs are relatively new.

While there is much to gain from working with another organization, whether within a sector or across sectors, it makes the management of activity significantly more complex. Standard operating procedures must be synchronized, and financial practices must not conflict. Human resources practices may require adjustment, and performance measures must be coordinated. Managing partnerships is hard, so the potential rewards should justify this greater effort.

CSPs are even more challenging than single-sector partnerships, however, because the individual partners frequently operate under significantly different legal and regulatory frameworks and have different missions, standard operating procedures, and measures of success. Yet the use of CSPs continues to expand because they have been successful in meeting challenges and accomplishing objectives that single organizations and conventional partnerships have not been able to address. In this context, the definition of CSPs that we find most useful is "a voluntary collaboration between organizations from two or more sectors that leverage their respective teams and resources to achieve mutually agreed-upon and measurable goals."[4]

These partnerships are most likely to succeed when the interests of the partners converge on the same project, program, enterprise, or activity, and when partners share fairly, if not equally, the investment, effort, risks, and rewards connected with the partnership. The most effective cross-sector partners make important decisions collaboratively. And perhaps most important, the partners communicate constantly and treat one another respectfully and as equal partners.

The structure of cross-sector partnerships varies widely, depending on the overall objective, the anticipated scope of the endeavor, and the longevity and location of operations. The roles that partners play in the partnership generally fit into one of three categories—funder, implementer, or stakeholder. *Funders* can come from all three sectors; can be large or small; can come in early, late, or throughout the process; and may or may not expect to get a return on their investment (or even to get their investment back at all—as with a grant or gift, for example). *Implementers* are the partners doing the work on the project, and all partners could potentially do some of the implementation activities. *Stakeholders* often make up the largest group of partners and include those affected by the partnership's actions; this group may include but is not limited to recipients (customers, clients, patients, or members); the local communities, neighborhoods, and places where the partnership operates; and those affected by the partnership activities, regardless of location.

The structure of the activity carried out by the partnership varies widely. The activity can carry the name of one partner and operate in a physical or virtual location through a *unitary* structure, in which the other partners provide funding and/or operational expertise. A conglomerate in the private sector or an authority in the public sector might be an example of a unitary structure. An activity that carries the name and operations of multiple partners can be identified as a *joint* initiative—for example, a business-improvement district could be considered a joint initiative.

Partners can also choose to create a *new* identity operated by one or more of the partners with existing and/or new personnel and systems. Under this model, the partners work together to create an organization focused on the partnership mission, which is entirely separate from that of their respective organizations. This structure enables the partners to operate as they did before the partnership and not have their management distracted from their independent responsibilities on a daily basis. An example of the new identity approach is a long-term franchise agreement to rehabilitate and operate a municipal water and wastewater system, which is governed by a board with members from each of the partners.

Another model is *partial* integration, where partners might choose to consolidate part or all of their separate administrative divisions, operations, legal, engineering, or technology and back office support. This model enables each partner to preserve its independence and identity while also saving time and money and improving management focus by consolidating activities that all partners consider support functions. An example of the partial integration model might be the consolidation of data storage and billing services for multiple partners that are collaboratively operating a long-term care facility for the elderly. Another version of partial integration is where each partner separates a portion of its existing operation to create a new organization focused on the partnership mission; for example, a job-placement company operated collaboratively by service trade unions, a construction company, and a nonprofit focused on helping public assistance recipients transition to self-supporting employment.

Finally, an *umbrella* structure might function best when the partners come together to carry out partnership activities periodically, but frequently enough and for work important enough that the umbrella vehicle is separate, permanently staffed, and prepared to become operational on a moment's notice. An example is an emergency services organization comprised of independent partners from all three sectors and multiple locations, which come together under an incident command structure to deal with a natural disaster, security crisis, or other predetermined event of significant consequence.

SUCCESSFUL PARTNERSHIPS ARE BUILT UPON A SHARED STRATEGY

Consensus on a mission and a detailed "road map" showing how to achieve that mission is the foundation of any successful partnership. Once the mission and critical path to it are formalized, partners can then focus on the most effective management mechanisms to get the work accomplished. A benchmarking exercise can be a very useful first step, as there is much to be learned from how other partnerships or independent organizations have sought to meet similar challenges. The process others have used to develop their strategy, for example, can help in mission definition. Benchmarking can also provide a framework for encouraging engagement and participation among the partners and can stimulate creative brainstorming to identify new ways of thinking about persistent problems.

Equally important, potential partners should only consider a partnership as a management option after they have conducted their own strategic planning. Only once an organization has a clear vision of its current and future mission, an inventory of its core strengths, and an accurate assessment of its weaknesses, can it find the best partners to achieve maximum results.

If the need for a partnership is determined and the appropriate partners are convened, the partners can then use a theory-of-change logic model to visually depict and determine their mutually desired outcomes and impacts.[5] Once those outcomes are identified, the partners can work backwards to create a road map to success, beginning with inputs, then working their way toward the necessary activities to measure the outputs that result in the desired impacts. When this analysis is complete, partners can begin to build a comprehensive strategic plan for the partnership.

A strategic plan for the partnership ensures a proper analysis of the impact of the partnership activities on the existing independent operations of each partner. This analysis looks at the possible interactions between services and goods produced by each partner, the potential effect of both on the partnership outputs, and the areas where those services and goods are being sourced and provided. The partners should carry out a value-chain analysis in order to map out and more accurately assess how these new activities might impact the process by which the partners have—and will bring—value to its customers. A value-chain analysis can assess the impact of the partnership on each partner's supply chain and on the customers and communities where the transactions take place.

CSPs generally make sense for larger-scale initiatives that have an implementation timeline of three years or more. Therefore, a comprehensive strategic-planning process will require extensive research and planning stages, particularly if the location (or locations) of the customer (and supply chain) are in challenging socioeconomic, political, or environmental sites. This pre-implementation work takes time and money but is essential to the success of a CSP. This may seem obvious, but because of the initial investment of time and money, it is often not done and thus reduces the value created by the partnership.

KEY ELEMENTS OF SUCCESSFUL CROSS-SECTOR PARTNERSHIP MANAGEMENT

Good management is essential to the success of any organization, regardless of sector. However, without exceptionally good management, the success of a CSP is impossible. Key elements of good management are similar, but several management tools are essential for effective CSPs—namely, collaborative leadership, diverse teams, innovative financing, quantifiable measures of success, and advanced communication and feedback mechanisms.[6]

Effective leadership is a key to success in any organization, but *collaborative leadership* is required for cross-sector partnerships. All effective leaders present a clear vision of success. Collaborative leaders reach out to and engage partners, customers, affected communities, and other key stakeholders in shaping that vision to ensure its outcomes and impacts provide maximum benefits to all affected parties.

To accomplish such a complex task, collaborative leaders focus on communication. They are active listeners, articulate speakers, and respectful of differences in culture, gender, ethnicity, beliefs, and professions. They are also willing not only to delegate authority but to make decisive decisions when necessary. Collaborative leaders use persuasion rather than power. Their authority comes from their expert knowledge, their commitment to shared success, and their personal integrity.

A *team management* approach is essential for CSPs given the diverse set of skills and knowledge required to accomplish the complex objectives they are to achieve. Teams should reflect the diversity of the organizations they represent, the customers they serve, and the communities in which they work.

To succeed, teams should have stable membership and be kept together long enough to develop trust and cohesion. Team members need to have clear roles and responsibilities, as well as the time to cross-train, so that they can fill in for one another as necessary. Over time, teams can develop a deep knowledge of the partners they are drawn from, along with the challenges faced by those partners, so that collective success increases as they learn together, assignment by assignment.[7] Team leaders should lead collaboratively if they are to maximize the performance of diverse teams.

Innovative financing techniques are characteristic of successful CSPs. These partnerships often form when conventional organizations using traditional financing methods are unable to meet important and complex challenges. Tiered financing structures are frequently required. Foundations, gifts, or government grants come first to fund preliminary research and planning. This is high-risk, speculative funding, and it is best if these funds do not need to be repaid, since participants are unsure at this stage whether the project will go forward. Social Impact Bonds (SIBs) and program-related investments (PRIs) can fund the pilot phase. This activity is less risky, but investors understand that if the pilot is not successful, they might lose their investment; conversely, they know that if the pilot is successful, they will not only be repaid but can get a competitive return as well. Partner organizations need to contribute funds, personnel, and in-kind assets. Once the activity is up and running, funding comes from customers (including any public funds that customers and service providers may be eligible to receive). Capital requirements may be met through a mix of public, private, and philanthropic sources.

As we have noted repeatedly, you can't manage what you can't measure.[8] This is especially true for CSPs. In these partnerships, two or more organizations come together with a preexisting vision, mission, and history, along with a set of stakeholders and a set of *quantifiable measures of success*. They come together, often for the first time, to do something they probably have not done before and for a new set of stakeholders. It is crucial that the partners focus on reaching consensus regarding how they will define and measure success, where they will get the necessary data, and how they will track and report results. They must identify the targets they will use, how those targets will be adjusted over time, and how the partners will hold themselves accountable (see chapter 5).

All organizations need *advanced communication and feedback* mechanisms to survive, improve, and succeed. These tools are crucial for CSPs because they bring together an extremely broad set of stakeholders, some who have interests in the current activities of the individual partners and some who are new stakeholders created by the partnership. Partnerships often attract and engage a broad range of diverse constituencies, including existing and new customers and suppliers and multiple funders with very different interests. Communities affected by these partnerships will express both positive and negative views of the partnership. A bias toward maximum communication and a sincere and ongoing commitment to transparency— achieved through the use of technology, including social media and communications platforms, both customized and generally accessible—can enable the partnership to obtain feedback from customers, other stakeholders, and even opponents that is essential to improving performance.

THE POTENTIAL OF CROSS-SECTOR PARTNERSHIPS

Cross-sector partnerships are relatively new, but they have already proven to be an effective management tool to meet challenges and to take advantage of opportunities beyond the capacity of a single organization—or even multiple organizations—from the same sector. Leaders and managers must recognize that organizing and implementing activities through such a complex mechanism takes additional time to accomplish the necessary preliminarily research and pre-planning. Additionally, leaders and managers must develop trust, negotiate terms and structures with one or more partners, agree upon measures of success, and get to work. Both manager and employee will need to learn new skills to partner successfully. In sum, CSPs have enormous potential but require both a great deal of hard work and a complex combination and coordination of assets to succeed.

PART III
THE ORGANIZATION AND SOCIETY

10

MARKETING, STAKEHOLDER RELATIONS, AND PUBLIC ENGAGEMENT

Improving Management Communications

Technological innovations beginning in late twentieth century and advancing in the first two decades of the twenty-first century have dramatically increased the speed and reach of communications while simultaneously reducing the price of transmission to near zero marginal cost. People today are spending more time looking at their smart phones than ever, often engaging in conversations on social media, shopping, or following their favorite celebrities online. This is both an opportunity and an obstacle in terms of organizational communication. Our customers, stakeholders, subordinates, peers, and supervisors are potentially almost always reachable, but they are also almost always distracted.

Despite the challenges, effective communication is a key element of leadership and management. According to Max Weber, charismatic leadership arises from the ability to speak well and to impart the words and emotion to inspire and create a sense of identification with followers.[1] And two of Peter Drucker's four skills for leaders to master are listening and communicating.[2] But the modern scope of organizational communications involves more than speaking and listening. Senior management must ensure that the following areas of specialization are covered: public information and media relations, marketing and branding, interpersonal communications, interviewing, negotiations, performance appraisals and coaching, and managing social media.

PUBLIC INFORMATION AND MEDIA RELATIONS

While it can sometimes seem that the media is only interested in your organization when something has gone wrong, in reality, the media (including social media) is essential to the survival and success of your organization, as it is the primary source of information about your organization for customers, potential customers, investors, regulators, donors, elected officials, and the rest of the media.

It is never fun to deal with news that reflects poorly on your organization, but without your input, the media reports will likely be worse than if your perspective were missing. Since the media is seldom going to call to ask what is going well in your operation, it is imperative that senior management prioritize pushing out positive information. Media relations and public information should also be a top priority since most organizations have legal obligations to report on their finances and other issues that affect the general public. Making communication a top priority requires the following: appointing a public information officer, developing and promulgating standard operating procedures for media relations, and building a communications strategy.

Having one point of contact for external requests for information is essential to success. It is not easy to force the vast array of media and other external inquiries through one central point, but it is worth trying. Equally difficult is to convince individuals throughout the organization not to respond directly, particularly "off the record." Nevertheless, continuing to reinforce the importance of following this process will benefit the organization generously over time and result in more accurate information for the media and their audiences.

Building a communications strategy should start with the formation of a team of employees who have experience dealing with the media and knowledge of the organization's overall vision and strategy. A good plan of any kind includes clear goals, measures for success, a timeline, contingent strategies for crises and the unexpected and an overall theme to connect all the initiatives together. That said, possible goals for a communications strategy include increasing public awareness and name recognition, raising funds, influencing news coverage, influencing public policy and/or regulation, retaining and recruiting customers, finding new employees, recruiting employees and/or volunteers, and improving the organization's image, including its record of positive social impact.

MARKETING AND BRANDING

Marketing and branding are often thought of in the context of private, for-profit organizations focused on selling goods and services. Nevertheless, most nonprofit and government organizations have customers, stakeholders, or clients to whom they provide services, while also competing with organizations from all three sectors for the same customers or clients. In many countries, all levels of education, health care, transportation, recreation, and even dispute resolution are provided by organizations from all three sectors that compete for students, patients, riders, recreators, and litigants.

Regardless of sector or service, all good marketing efforts begin with a strategic plan. Within that plan, there should be a clear message, identification of the target audience, and an advertising campaign based on your brand.[3] Successful marketing plans are focused on the ideal customer, have a compelling message for your brand of product or service, and use the media channel (or channels) that best reach your ideal customer.

Branding is the process by which an organization creates a unique identity conveying the utility, quality, and intrinsic value of its product, service, or package of products and services. In many respects, an effective marketing plan is focused as much on your brand as it is on a particular product or service. Branding seeks to create immediate recognition in the marketplace for what makes your goods and services more valuable than those of your competitors. Effective branding also signals to your current and potential customers what they can expect from your organization.[4]

A valuable and recognized brand begins with offering a high-quality service or product at a fair price. The brand is then built through advertising, an easily recognized logo and slogan, excellent customer service, promotional materials, and, over time, a great reputation. Branding helps an organization reach and then hold on to customers, who, in turn, will recommend your organization to others. A strong brand commands a price premium and attracts investors and partners. A respected brand also attracts the best employees, increases their motivation to succeed, gives them a greater sense of pride in and affirmation of the importance of their work, and thereby deepens their loyalty to the organization.

Having a well-known brand simplifies communication to new and existing customers. It can also help create a more targeted and thus more effective advertising campaign.[5] A well-positioned and clearly communicated brand meets a recognized customer need, is understood by customers, and enables customers to reach their goals by acquiring your product or service. Finally, a critical component to brand success is building social networks. And a key element in building social networks is managing social media.

MANAGING SOCIAL MEDIA

Social media has disrupted advertising, media, politics, international affairs, and organizational communications. Social media enables politicians, entrepreneurs, advocates, and others with an agenda to go around traditional media, political parties, and other stakeholders by "speaking directly" to their supporters and the not-yet-converted. Social media actors create their own brands, lifestyles, comedy, religions, movements, and markets. For organizations, social media sites can also be more effective than traditional methods at finding new employees.

Social media can create new spokespersons for an organization (often individuals that do not work for the organization, at least until they become too influential not to hire . . .). It can also provide new and often more effective communication channels, which are perfectly aligned to the target demographic for the product or service. New media venues often significantly reduce the cost of marketing and customer relations, more rapidly transmit important information, build stronger customer loyalty and greater levels of satisfaction, and increase the regularity of communication with customers and stakeholders.

Top management plays a key role in the use and success of social media as a communications tool. But while managers often find the benefits of social media obvious, they often underestimate the risks. For one, it can provide a forum for dissatisfied customers and employees, for sabotage by competitors, and for conflicting messaging from various actors within the organization. Second, it makes the organization vulnerable to failing to keep its social media information current, accurate, and polished. As is true with other key elements of management, accurate measurement of the benefits and costs of the use of social media is critical to the successful use of this powerful communications tool.[6]

The use of social media for organizational communication is still evolving. It seems clear that it has dramatically changed the cost structure of marketing and advertising and has expanded the potential market for private and social organizations. It has also expanded the opportunities for organizations to communicate inside and outside the organization. In addition, social media has created more feedback from customers and stakeholders, and that feedback often comes immediately after the related interaction between the organization and the customer. Social media has also made it much easier for customers, citizens, interest groups, communities, and terrorists to talk among themselves, reach and promulgate their own conclusions, and advocate for change (or for the status quo or even for past practices).[7] The barriers to entry for social media access are low, but gaining attention on these media is a constantly evolving craft.

INTERPERSONAL COMMUNICATION SKILLS

Every leader and manager can increase their effectiveness by improving their communication skills. Reading books on the subject, taking courses and attending training sessions, hiring a communications coach, and seeking guidance from those you know as excellent communicators can all help. In our view, becoming a better communicator involves three skills— listening, mastering the feedback process, and questioning and responding.[8]

Listening is much more than not talking. It is a way to gather information, learn, build trust, earn loyalty, and encourage collaboration. Effective listening requires outward signs that you are paying attention to the speaker—behavior that is generally called *attending behavior* and includes nonverbal cues. "Attending" behaviors include occasional encouraging words, silent attention, and questions when appropriate. Finally, effective listeners summarize and paraphrase what was said to make sure they understand and to let the speaker know they were really paying attention.

Effective feedback focuses on things that can be changed productively rather than criticism regarding personal traits or the speaker's background. The best feedback is delivered privately and in a timely manner (not immediately, in the moment of the incident, but within a day or two). It works best if you encourage others to provide feedback on your own actions as well. Feedback should also be focused on one behavior (even if you think there are several that need to change) and, if at all possible, it should mix some positive feedback with a message that a certain behavior should be modified. Combining active listening with these effective feedback methods will increase the chances that your messages will be heard and the desired modifications will take place while also letting you maintain positive workplace relationships with your subordinates, peers, and supervisors. Being self-aware, self-critical, and open to feedback yourself can only improve overall organizational communications.

Questioning and responding techniques can also contribute to more positive communication from senior management. Asking open questions can enable the questioner to obtain more information from the person being questioned, and it generally reveals more about the priorities and opinions of the person responding to the question. For the responder, a less structured question is often less confrontational and gives them the freedom to say what they want to say in their own way. Open questions facilitate organizational communication.

INTERVIEWING

Interviewing, negotiations, performance appraisals, and coaching are four of the most common and important contexts in which communications skill are crucial to achieving beneficial outcomes. A thorough discussion of each area could easily fill a chapter or even a book, so we will focus on the highlights of each and suggest other sources for those interested in a deeper dive into the subject. For the area of interviewing, we will focus on the contexts of job interviews and on being interviewed by the media.

For many managers, interviewing candidates for a position is one of their least favorite parts of the job. It takes a lot of time, you have to cover the same ground over and over again with different candidates (many of whom you may quickly decide are not right for the position), and in the end, you either choose the candidate you thought you would choose before the process began or you find it difficult to choose between three or more candidates. To make the process less painful and more productive, consider the following steps.

First, make sure you have a clear statement of why the position is a great opportunity for the candidate and an equally clear assessment of what factors will determine the best candidate.

Second, have the same set of questions for every candidate, predominately open-ended ones that focus the candidate on the skills needed to succeed in the position and the interpersonal behaviors that are likely to contribute to success. Third, create a scorecard of skills and behaviors for the position and use the candidate's answers and resume to fill in the boxes next to each desired skill and behavior. Placing numerical values on each can help you weigh the relative importance of each category and enable you to compare your assessments of all the candidates under consideration.

A completely different type of interview you may have to face is one in which you or someone else in the organization is interviewed by the media. This is a great opportunity for an organization and its representative being interviewed; however, it is high risk as well. While there is no way to guarantee a failproof interview, through many years of experience and research, we have identified several factors that enable its success. It begins with honoring the interview deadline; make yourself available well in advance of their deadline, or respectfully decline with a good explanation.

Never lie or stretch the truth, and be as transparent as possible. As we have seen so often in all three sectors, the "cover-up" is often much more damaging than the incident itself. Be lively and sincere—if you aren't excited about what your organization is doing, why would the audience care? Remember to say the name of your organization as often as possible and use "we" instead of "I," unless it is to take responsibility for something negative.

Answer each question directly and then stop talking. Being succinct projects competence and precision. If possible, go into the interview with three key points, and no matter what you are asked, include at least one of the three key points in your answer.

NEGOTIATIONS

Negotiation skills are beneficial in almost every aspect of life—being a good parent, having a successful marriage, buying or renting a place to live or a car to drive, getting a menu item without some of the ingredients, or even agreeing on what movie, play, or concert to attend. At work, negotiating skills play an important role in budget allocations, contracting, salaries and benefits, union and labor relations, customer satisfaction and warranties, regulatory compliance, tax application and enforcement, partnerships, and many other aspects of management and supervision. Negotiation is a profession itself with many complex layers; those with the interest and need can read any number of excellent books on the topic, attend an executive training session or a college course, or even earn a certification or degree.[9] In the context of this book, we can provide several broad considerations and suggestions for negotiation.

As a senior manager, you should prepare for any work situation where the other party may consider the topic under discussion as negotiable, even if you initially view it as your decision alone. You need to consider how important your relationship is with the other party and how long the relationship is likely to continue. You should also consider the consequences of resolving the situation without conflict and the degree to which a compromise would impact your organization's overall ability to achieve its mission.

If you can accommodate the concerns of the other party without compromising your desired outcome, you can get the job done and possibly deepen an important relationship. If the outcome does not materially impact the ability of the organization to perform, you might consider simply agreeing to the other party's requests. And if the issue is not pressing at all, you might just delay dealing with it.

If the issue must be dealt with and the position of each party seems nonnegotiable, consider the Relational Identity Theory developed by Daniel Shapiro.[10] Shapiro's simple but powerful methodology includes several important principles: aiming for harmony instead of victory, recognizing that the path to harmony may not be linear, incorporating both the past and future in a resolution, and recognizing that resolution may require both emotional and structural transformation. Shapiro's methodology may not fit your negotiation situation perfectly, but we have found his process helpful as a starting point for dealing with even the most difficult negotiations.

PERFORMANCE APPRAISALS

Most large and many medium-sized organizations operate performance appraisal systems to promote constructive dialogue and ensure accountability. Sadly, in many cases, these systems very rapidly devolve into a mountain of meaningless paperwork for all concerned. Too often, busy managers and leaders ask their team members to establish their own job descriptions, report their performance, do a self-assessment, and then send the completed form to the boss for a signature (often signed by a machine and executed by the executive assistant).

The reasons for such ineffectiveness include the presence of unions and labor-management agreements that supersede the appraisal system, the absence of consequences for a good or bad appraisal, and a culture that leads to "everyone's great" or "everyone's satisfactory." The reality is also that most important work is done by teams and, therefore, one's individual performance is important only in the context of the success or failure of the team.

Jack Welch, the legendary CEO of General Electric (GE), sought to give consequences to his appraisal system meaning by forcing managers to put employees into performance categories by percentages, with the top 10 percent getting big raises and stock options and the bottom 10 percent being fired. Ultimately, GE abandoned the system when they found large numbers in the "second best" category leaving because they viewed themselves as the best (and other employers thought so too). Additionally, they found that many of the bottom 10 percent had been compromised by bad supervisors or a time-limited personal circumstance such as an illness or a family tragedy.

In our experience, the performance management systems described in chapter 5 are more effective tools for motivating the individual and the organization as a whole to do their best. Performance management coupled with individualized, detailed job descriptions; standard operating procedures; recruitment practices that find the best person for each job; the encouragement and empowerment of teams; and ongoing training can achieve better results than performance appraisals and can do so without as much bureaucracy and paperwork. For more targeted individual-performance improvement, we suggest an annual self-assessment coupled with on-the-job coaching from the individual's immediate supervisor.

COACHING

Senior managers have long turned to professional coaches to improve their skills and job performance. For first-line managers, line employees, and other staff reporting to more senior managers, a professional coach is generally not affordable and might lack the specificity and organizational knowledge to provide meaningful feedback. Turning an often bureaucratic and unproductive performance appraisal session into an in-house coaching program could be a low- or no-cost adaptive reuse of resources with a huge potential upside. Using an individual self-assessment as a baseline, managers can coach their direct reports into self-improvement and better performance.

Coaching sessions should begin with the self-assessment and with praise for all of the positive efforts of the individual. A discussion should follow about what can be improved, coupled with a plan for training to facilitate that improvement. Following the initial session, the manager should check in regularly, in person when possible, and by email, text, and phone to provide feedback and help and to express positive support. To make sure items do not fall through the cracks and that both parties remain on the same page, written summaries of all communication between the individual and the coach should be shared and confirmed by both parties.

INTRAORGANIZATIONAL COMMUNICATION

Senior management often treats intraorganizational communication as necessary but seldom all that important. We should keep our employees informed, but it need not be systematic or polished. Supervisors will take care of the job-specific communications, while various divisions—human resources, legal, safety, operations—will handle whatever messaging is required by law or regulation. This approach changed in organizations participating in the waves of Total Quality Management

(TQM) adoptions in the 1990s and the very similar Lean Management movement in the twenty-first century.

Organizations implementing TQM and Lean Management emphasized that enhanced intraorganizational communication would improve employee-senior leadership relations, enrich communications between workers, and heighten positive perceptions of organizational support.[11] Other studies have shown that effective intraorganizational communication can promote positive safety attitudes in hospitals.[12] Communication provides crucial information about one's job and relationships to others in the organization, builds trust, provides situational awareness, helps problem-solving, aids retention, increases socialization, and enhances motivation.

In the nineteenth and early twentieth centuries, intraorganizational communication was viewed as primarily top-down, using Frederick Taylor's principles of scientific management and Max Weber's ideal bureaucracy. Later in the twentieth century, internal-communication theorists focused on motivating through leadership, relationship-building through teams, and developing multidirectional communication with feedback loops such as in TQM.

More recently, those seeking to improve intraorganizational communications focus on creating a culture of communication whereby multiple channels of communication, both formal and informal, written and visual, scheduled and issue-specific, and top-down as well as bottom-up seek to create a networked organization. Clearly, email and social media play an important role in helping to create a more open and continuous flow of official communication within the organization. In addition, senior managers must make time for as much face-to-face communication as possible.

Some other key attributes of an effective intraorganizational communications strategy include providing information in a timely fashion, championing an open and transparent culture, encouraging participation in all levels of the organization, and recognizing and rewarding important contributions. Successful communication is, by definition, a multidirectional process. And, as with virtually every important aspect of management, measurement of the effectiveness of the intraorganizational communications strategy is essential to its success.[13]

PERSONAL COMMUNICATION

Email and social media enable senior managers to communicate with virtually anyone, anywhere, at any time, and at virtually no cost. This ease and speed of communication enabled some leaders to become international celebrities—a brand themselves and extremely influential. On the other side, the potential tendency to overcommunicate has cost others their careers and even led to legal jeopardy when comments from years before resurfaced.

Therefore, extreme caution is advised. Before you click Send, reflect on the reality that the message you send could be forwarded around the globe within seconds or even ten years in the future. It will be virtually impossible to take back. And it will exist for your entire life and probably after your death. In most instances, even somewhat controversial views or humor might be better left unsaid.

Finally, least you forget, most people carry a smart phone with a camera and a recorder. So always be careful with what you say and do. You never know who is watching, listening, or reading.

11

ORGANIZATIONAL ETHICS

We believe that principles matter. Organizations lacking an ethical compass are, by definition, poorly managed. But not everyone agrees with us. Some senior managers view ethics as a relatively short list of positive and negative behaviors for their employees. Leadership will reward or punish these behaviors to the degree to which they contribute to the organization's success in achieving its mission, but ethics is not perceived as essential to effective leadership and management.

We believe that organizational ethics is a management fundamental that contributes substantially to long-term success. When organizational ethics are absent (or poorly defined and communicated), it can create an ethical vacuum, culminating in a downward spiral of organizational decisions and behaviors that ultimately destroy the organization. It is the responsibility of senior management to create an ethical culture, reinforced with an accountability system that helps guide their organization to an ethical and economically sustainable future.[1]

Senior managers who ignore the importance of an ethical culture are in imminent danger of a disastrous product-liability case, a class-action lawsuit, a customer revolt, a deluge of bad press, severe damage to their reputations, and loss of their jobs, if not their careers.

Establishing an organizational code of ethics is a good first step in the right direction. Adding a list of core values to guide the organization toward the strategic plan and other important official documents is also helpful. In this chapter, we present some of the most common and important areas where ethics are an essential tool for organizational success, remembering that it takes time to develop an ethical culture and a great deal of work to maintain it.

HOW ARE ORGANIZATIONAL ETHICS ESTABLISHED AND COMMUNICATED?

Organizations exist in community, cultural, national, and global contexts, each with its own traditions, laws, regulations, religions, and social norms. The intellectual roots of organizational ethics generally reflect the thinking of English utilitarians John Stuart Mill and Jeremy Bentham that, in any given circumstance, the moral high ground is achieved when the greatest good is achieved for the greatest number of people. The challenge presented by this thinking is in how we define and measure "good."[2] While there will always be debate over the meaning of "good," without a discussion of the definition of good the organization can easily dismiss morality as irrelevant. The risk of an amoral or immoral organization is greater if there is no debate over ethics or the "public interest." In terms of organizational ethics, utilitarianism is useful in that it values good for collective over individual benefit.

In the twentieth century, philosopher John Rawls argued that conflict inevitably arises in society and, thereby, in organizations due to resource constraints.[3] Rawls rejected utilitarianism because he believed that there are basic human rights that must be guaranteed to all and never compromised. Therefore, he constructed a two-tiered theory of ethics based on justice. Primary in this theory is equal liberty, requiring that certain basic rights be guaranteed to and protected for all persons. A practical illustration of this principle is the United Nations Declaration of Human Rights.[4] The declaration's second principle asserts that each person should have a fair and equal opportunity to official positions and jobs but that, recognizing that inequalities will always exist, priority must be given to meeting the needs of those who are disadvantaged. Balancing individual rights and collective equality is a worthy quest, but one that most organizations will continue to find a struggle.

In the twenty-first century, many organizations are either global, participate in partnerships, or have contracts in many different locations throughout the world. Additionally, organizations often employ a wide range of professionals—doctors, lawyers, engineers, scientists, MBAs, MPAs—each with their own professional codes of ethics and values. Senior management must navigate through this complex landscape, focused on principles, values, and behaviors that are essential to the organization's reputation and sustainable success while also seeking to minimize dissonance among the various ethical codes to which their employees are committed.

We have identified eight major ethical issues that most organizations should address. Senior management should ensure that all employees are aware of the importance of these issues and how they are expected to act when confronted with choices involving these ethical concerns. In many cases, there will be no clear right or wrong choice. Therefore, organizations should learn from the outcomes of the choices its members make in these ethical situations and provide ongoing information and case studies with the goal of improving the collective organizational ethical behavior.[5]

CORRUPTION

Corruption as a major ethical concern is not new or likely to disappear soon. At the same time, international recognition of the problem continues to rise, and behaviors that were once tolerated or even rewarded (particularly if it won contracts and jobs) are now almost universally disparaged. Corruption increases costs; deepens inequality; undermines trust in our institutions, organizations, laws, and leaders; and diminishes an organization's capacity to carry out its mission and achieve its goals.

Transparency International defines corruption as, "the abuse of entrusted power for private gain."[6] Corruption includes bribery at the highest levels of public and private organizations to secure contracts, regulatory approvals, access to public lands and natural resources, and other financial benefits outside of legal processes and in conflict with the rule of law. It also includes actions by individuals for personal gain, including fraud and embezzlement, in-kind benefits to friends and family, personal use of corporate assets, kickbacks, bribes to expedite the processing of a license or passport, placement fees, and stock speculation (such as insider trading).

To minimize corruption, senior managers must require training and education on the laws and regulations that apply to government transactions in countries where their organization operates. Senior managers should set an example by avoiding transactions with organizations often involved in questionable practices. Transparency in financial transactions is extremely important, so avoid transactions that do not identify the key individuals involved in the activity.

Senior managers should also carefully review the impact of its performance management incentives to assure that they do not pressure staff to engage in kickbacks or other gifts or benefits to meet unreasonably high sales targets. Managers must also be mindful that pressures to reduce costs could lead purchasing agents to influence suppliers to sacrifice quality or safety in an effort to drive down prices. Senior managers should also create a culture that encourages employees to report what appear to be corrupt practices in the workplace, even when they are not legally required to do so.

A comprehensive anticorruption strategy should include a code of conduct with legal requirements for proper behavior. Education and training programs communicating the negative consequences of corruption for the individual, the organization, the community, and for customers, suppliers, and society at large can help create motivation to combat corruption. Finally, a reporting mechanism, including a confidential communication channel is a key component in an effective anticorruption program.

CONFLICTS OF INTEREST

A conflict of interest can occur when a member of the organization has an undisclosed financial interest in a company seeking a contract, partnership, or financial benefit from the member's employer (or is in a position of authority, such as a board member, outside counsel, or a financial advisor). Such a person is in a position where they might well choose to benefit their personal interest to the detriment of the organization.

A similar conflict could occur when an organizational member deals with an outside organization, particularly a paid contractor, and a close friend or family member might benefit from the relationship. Kickbacks of payments to the contractor to the purchaser can turn a potential conflict of interest into a crime.

Conflicts of interest can also arise when a member or senior manager develops an ongoing and substantial contractual relationship with a supplier or partner. Such an individual might hold an explicit or implied expectation that, at some point, the supplier or partner will hire them or otherwise provide a financial reward. This situation is so common that it is regularly referred to as a revolving door (for example, a procurement officer in the military retires and then is hired as a senior executive at a weapons supplier to the military).

There are a number of tools available to mitigate conflicts of interest. An employer can require employees in a position to influence financial decisions or partnerships to disclose the financial investments of those employees and even the financial investments of their immediate and extended families. Those disclosure filings might require annual updates.

Organizations can and should prohibit employees from participating in any relationship where an employee has a financial interest. Alternatively, the organization should require pre-approval by a supervisor when there might be an appearance of conflict of interest. A less strict policy could provide a periodic peer review of an employee's decisions in relation to their private interests and investments. Another more flexible policy could require employees to file an annual report on their outside interests and those of their family that might be perceived as a potential conflict of interest. Some employers (particularly the government) might place one- or two-year restrictions on an employee seeking a position in an organization that benefitted substantially from that employee's decisions while they were in their current position.

EQUAL OPPORTUNITY

Regardless of the law, many ethical organizations commit themselves to merit-based policies on employment, promotion, and evaluation. The operation of those policies might be as specific as mandating objective tests, which are common in many public civil service systems. More common policies might simply mandate transparent and publicly accessible job descriptions that state the jobs' required education levels, licenses, years of experience, computer skills, languages, and even physical abilities.

Organizations fully committed to equal opportunity will welcome candidates from inside and outside the organization. To recruit and maintain a diverse workforce, organizations will publicly affirm their commitment to equal opportunity. To ensure objectivity and openness, an organization might retain an outside consultant to manage critical job searches.

To assure stakeholders (including those in the local communities where the organization maintains offices and facilities) that you are committed to equal opportunity, you should use open processes for procurement, partnerships, and business opportunities as often as possible. Giving local small businesses a chance to compete for contracts can provide very positive publicity for the organization. Local sourcing can also ensure reliable and timely delivery, and can often provide a better value when all factors are considered. Building an organization's reputation on merit-based employment and purchasing is good business, no matter what business you are in. It can also be helpful in times of crisis when your decision-making is called into question. And in more and more locations, equal opportunity is not only ethical; it is a legal requirement.

WORKPLACE JUSTICE

An ethical organization will provide a version of due process in handling discipline and complaints. Such a process is important to an organization regardless of whether supervisors themselves are handling discipline and complaints appropriately. In instances where some degree of interpersonal friction exists between an employee and supervisor, the employee should have the right to an independent appeal. And for senior management, an appeal process can help ensure that similar situations are assessed and handled consistently across the organization.

Employees should also have a complaint process available outside their chain of command. Operated by the human resources department or a more independent ombudsman, such a process should enable employees to raise concerns, whether personal or organization-related, without fear of punishment from their supervisor or even coworkers. Senior management benefits from such a process in that they become aware of even perceptions of problems before the rest of the organization and the outside world and can then fix the problem (or the perception of the problem) before serious damage is done to the organization.

Similarly, it makes sense to establish a secure and independent office to receive whistleblower concerns out of the normal chain of command and with a guarantee of confidentiality. A hotline for complaints about harassment of all kinds, including grants of anonymity, should also be provided. It is in the organization's best interests to learn about such concerns first and perhaps correct the problem before more serious and well-publicized events occur. Even if claims are invalid or exaggerated, the process will have at least given whistleblowers an opportunity to air their concerns.

Organizations should also accommodate personal issues in employee life, including childcare, mother and family leave for childbirth, care for elderly parents or partners, and care for physical and mental health issues. Related concerns should be handled with confidentiality, fairness, compassion, and empathy, even if not required by law or labor agreements. Organizations make substantial investments in recruitment and training, so supporting a staff person during hard times is not only just; it is good business, as a just workplace usually leads to a motivated and productive workforce.

PRIVACY AND SECURITY

Employees have a right to expect that their employer is extending its best efforts to ensure their physical, emotional, and cyber security, even beyond what is legally required. And employers have an ethical responsibility to ensure the safety of their employees while they are working. But safety is not just an ethical issue; a safe workplace is also a powerful recruitment and retention tool and mitigates potential legal liability.

To provide physical security, the workplace should limit building access to employees and those who have a legitimate reason to be admitted—that includes customers, suppliers, public officials, partners, media, and others authorized by members of the organization. Wherever possible, identification of those entering and leaving the workplace should be monitored and logged; weapons should be detected and not permitted in the workspace; and security personnel, both in uniform and in plain clothes, should be deployed whenever feasible.

Senior management must also ensure that the workplace is accessible and safe for those with physical challenges, which means including elevators of sufficient size for wheelchairs, ramps, guard rails, and desks and chairs with proper elevation (or adjustable furniture and workspaces). Safety equipment, including smoke and gas detectors, fire extinguishers, emergency lights, and backup generators should also be available at all locations.

Cybersecurity is a major responsibility of senior management. Customers, suppliers, and employees must trust your organization to protect any of their personal information that could be used by criminals to drain their bank accounts, run up their credit card balances, steal their identities, and possibly disrupt their lives. Here again, this is management's ethical responsibility, but it also has substantial consequences for the organization's survival.

A safe workplace also operates with strong anti-harassment policies that are vigorously enforced. A diverse workforce is often more creative and productive, and to maintain a diverse workforce, all members must feel confident that they will not be subjected to physical or verbal abuse for their ethnic origin, appearance, gender, religion, or views. Productive organizations also give employees sufficient personal space so that they can work free from the worry that others will impose behaviors on them that make them uncomfortable.

SUSTAINABILITY AND ENVIRONMENTAL STEWARDSHIP

Climate change and environmental degradation will likely continue as major challenges throughout the twenty-first century. Thus, senior managers have an ethical responsibility to adopt sustainable practices and to minimize the negative environmental impact of their operations. Organizations that consider ignoring this ethical responsibility will suffer the wrath of many soon-to-be-former customers and staff. Additionally, organizations that adopt sustainable practices often find that doing so makes them more efficient and profitable, while adding value to their branding and marketing initiatives.[7]

There are a number of steps organizations can take to reduce energy use and their carbon footprint. Developers of new office spaces in major cities see zero-energy facilities as important components of a first-class building. Organizations buying or leasing such spaces are not only behaving ethically but are also lowering their operating costs. Zero-energy rehabilitations are becoming more common in both large and smaller markets as energy-efficient building supplies are dropping in cost and increasing in supply. Wind, solar, and water power generators are also expanding in rural urban areas around the world as the price-per-kilowatt-hour continues to drop.

Recycling and reuse practices are also more widespread. In a number of cities around the world, government organizations are offering to supply solid waste "products" to private firms that will reuse, recycle, and transform—with minimal negative environmental impact—that solid waste into new products that have economic value.

Ethical organizations are also encouraging and even requiring their suppliers to use sustainable practices, such as minimizing packaging and using biodegradable materials. In addition, some organizations are converting their vehicle fleets to the least-damaging fuel sources and selecting delivery services that do the same thing. And some of these environmentally responsible agencies are also seeking to minimize the environmental impact of their employees' commutes. For example, environmentally concerned senior managers can subsidize employees using mass transit to commute to work. Organizations can also make it easy and acceptable to bike to work by providing places to change and shower, a more casual dress code, bike racks in and outside the facility, and gyms and subsidized gym memberships to help more employees to become fit enough to bike to work. Organizations with significant resources can also build and subsidize housing close to the workplace, enabling employees to live close enough to walk to work.

ECONOMIC JUSTICE

Increasing economic inequality poses a real danger to the stability and continued improvement of quality of life for every person on earth. While public policy may be required to achieve a reasonable level of economic justice, ethical organizations can begin to close the gap with a number of positive employee policies. As a starting point, ethical organizations can decide to go beyond the legally required minimum wage to paying a "living wage," so that an employee can afford to live a decent life within commuting distance.

Truly ethical organizations will assist lower-income workers with access to available government subsidies for housing and transportation, top off those benefits when necessary, or find other sources of subsidies or in-kind benefits, including organization funds. These ethical organizations will also ensure that every employee has a health insurance policy.

While many countries have social-security retirement systems, the benefits are seldom enough to support a decent retirement, even if health care benefits are heavily subsidized. Organization pension plans that provide a certain percentage salary increase based on the number of years worked (often referred to as defined benefit plans) are disappearing; however, ethical organizations provide some level of matching funds for employees who choose to invest a portion of their salary in some type of mutual fund or investment account.

Organizations committed to economic justice will also share the value of intellectual property developed by employees on the job. And they will protect that intellectual property for the employee and themselves even after the employee leaves the organization. These ethical organizations will also seek to ensure that there is diversity at all compensation levels and that there are no glass ceilings, policies, or practices blocking upward mobility based on personal characteristics. Organizations truly committed to economic justice will also seek to reduce the widening gap in compensation between senior management and the frontline employees who directly serve the organization's customers.

SOCIAL IMPACT

There are a growing number of leading academics, philanthropists, government officials, social organization executives, corporate CEOs, and even investment bankers who believe that income inequality has reached dangerous levels. Many of these leaders also believe that the absence of robust measurements of the social impact of our organizations often results in distorted assessments of their true value. For example, is a large and highly profitable fossil fuel or mining company a benefit to society or a net cost if you quantify and subtract the environmental and health damage they do but leave to others to address?

Social-impact measures seek to quantify the social benefit or cost of an organization's actions at the same level of accuracy and vigor as measures of its financial outcomes. Though relatively new, the field of social-impact measurement is developing rapidly as society expands its use of cross-sector partnerships to address our most pressing social challenges in the twenty-first century—income inequality, affordable housing, quality health care and education for all, a sustainable environment, and reversal of the increasingly dangerous weather patterns brought on by higher and higher levels of carbon in the atmosphere.

WHAT IS THE ROLE OF ETHICS IN EFFECTIVE MANAGEMENT?

In the globalized, hyperconnected world of the twenty-first century, all organizations must anticipate being held accountable to ever-higher standards of ethical behavior. And they must realize that the consequences of not meeting those standards will often go beyond a few days of negative media coverage. More and more customers are demanding a good price, high quality, and social responsibility. Often customers will refuse to patronize organizations that they believe are behaving unethically; similarly, they will gravitate toward organizations that market and deliver on their pursuit of ethical behavior.

Today's regulators are looking beyond their national borders to assess how companies, social organizations, and even their own government agencies are behaving, regardless of how lax local laws and regulators might be; however, organizations can no longer be satisfied with simply not breaking the law. Senior managers must also consider the justice of the laws themselves and consider holding themselves to a higher standard than the laws do, working to improve the justice of the society in which they operate. To do so, they must consider service to the public interest as a performance indicator and take responsibility for the impact of their organizations' operations on society.

12

THE FUTURE OF WORK

How Will Changes in Work and
Society Change Management?

Technology has changed economic life which, in turn, has changed the nature of work. In the pre-industrial era, most work involved manual labor with the goal of securing food, clothing, and shelter. Throughout the twentieth century, manual labor was replaced by machines. In the twenty-first century, we are in a brain-based economy, moving toward ever-increasing levels of automation.[1] In the United States, at this writing, 80 percent of our GDP is in the service sector.[2] Communication and information technology have made it possible for work to be increasingly disconnected from places of work.[3] While some service professions require brick-and-mortar locations, many services are delivered virtually, and much of the work required to deliver those services need not be completed on location.

Network management and the reduction of vertically integrated organizations have spread an organization's work among many physical locations. Barcodes, containerized shipping, air freight, inexpensive communication, and enhanced data storage have made just-in-time production more common and organizations more efficient.[4] And just-in-time production has reduced the need for storing and paying for inventory, thereby reducing the gap between incurring the cost of production and being paid for whatever is produced.

Managing vendors who are not co-located means that more management work takes place without face-to-face contact. Interactive communication is less common, replaced by rapid e-mails and text messages. More work is automated and workplace technology is constantly changing, requiring frequent training and learning, both on the job and back at school. Organizational change is now the norm, so standard operating procedures need constant adjustment due to the need to learn the benefits and operational requirements of new technologies. Information technology permits management access to real-time data on organizational performance, enabling and requiring constant adjustment in management direction and organizational behavior.[5]

Further, the growth of a global economy is causing the "shrinking" of the globe. People travel and communicate more than ever before. The needs of multinational organizations and an emerging global elite are having a profound impact on nations, communities, families, and people.[6] Globalization is diversifying workplaces and communities and splitting families geographically, as people seek professional advancement and individual self-actualization. Families that once provided direct in-person contact and support now use communication technology to stay in touch and send money to provide support. Instead of elderly parents living with their children, children often now subsidize care and housing for their parents. Anti-immigration impulses are typically dominated by the needs of commerce and the discovery that, despite our differences, humans share a large number of needs and traits.[7] Technology and economic change are fostering cultural changes that are easy to observe in daily life and in the modern workplace.

These evolving cultural and social norms are changing how we work as well. More of us work part time, as part of the gig economy, creating a new set of challenges for both managers and staff.[8] The growing role of women in the workplace and the drive for gender equality is also changing many patterns of organizational interaction. Civil rights and gay rights have also changed workplace behaviors. These changes are helping organizations become more productive and merit-based. The global economy and the growth of the brain-based economy is diversifying the demography of the best-managed organizations. The needs of childcare and elder care are requiring work schedules to become more flexible.[9] The declining social acceptability of rigid hierarchy is flattening organizational structures and increasing communication from staff to senior management.[10]

A highly mobile global economy is changing the impact of geography on work and increasing competition in both the public and private sectors. Cities compete globally to host businesses, tourists, meetings, and conventions. They work hard to attract residents, even if some homeowners occupy their high-end apartments only for a few weeks out of the year. This puts pressure on local government costs and organizational performance. Distinctly local character must be synched with more homogeneous global requirements. Foreign management and staff have become more common in the private sector, increasing the requirements to more actively communicate local rules and customs.

More work must be conducted in coordination with personnel, clients, and customers who are working and living in different time zones. Global supply chains can be interrupted by human-made and natural crises, so organizations must develop redundant backup systems to ensure work can be completed.[11] The drive for greater efficiency, automation, and differential wage structures in different nations reduce labor's bargaining power and threaten worker rights. Economic power outside the reach of national governments can challenge national sovereignty and even threaten democratic rule. This indirectly affects the nature of work by fostering more rapid evolution of workplace regulation to facilitate participation in the global economy. While there is some resistance to these changes, economic power tends to overwhelm this resistance.

Particularly in cultures that are built around work-life balance and that encourage life outside of the workplace, strains have become visible and obvious. Technology and the global economy mean that for some, work is now possible twenty-four hours a day, seven days a week. The internet, low-cost communication and information, and cloud computing mean that work can follow you wherever you go. You no longer need to commute to a workplace to do many of the tasks required to complete work.[12]

Still, anyone observing a modern office setting will see people scanning social media and shopping websites on frequent breaks between periods of work. The boundaries between home life and work also take place at work, as "work" time is devoted to recreation, games, social interaction, and other non-work activities. This is not always possible in every work setting, but it is possible in any place where creative or unstructured work is undertaken. Since outputs must still be produced in virtually every workplace, we don't think of this issue as particularly serious, but it can present management problems if non-work tasks crowd out work during the workday.

The larger problem is workaholism, where people are so obsessed with work, they become limited and one-dimensional. People must now self-consciously struggle to create boundaries between work and home. There is a great deal of professional pressure to breach those boundaries, and it is not clear what new norms will develop to facilitate work-life balance. Managers must learn to require staff to defer work. Without work-life balance, burnout and declining performance is probable.[13] Effective managers need to recognize the need for people to turn work off.

MANAGING IN A CHANGING WORK ENVIRONMENT

Rapidly changing technologies, societies, consumer behavior, and economic life create a set of profound challenges to managers. The stability of large-scale, vertically integrated hierarchies has been replaced by more frequent instability and disruption.[14] Where twentieth-century organizations were able to achieve decades of dominance and depend on reasonably predictable external environments, the rate of organizational change and challenge has accelerated throughout the twenty-first century. And we see nothing that will slow this rate of change.

Modern managers need to constantly collect, analyze, and understand information about their organization and the environment it operates in. Strategies must be constantly reassessed and modified in the light of new information. Our ability to collect and communicate information has expanded exponentially, but the human capacity to learn and change cannot possibly grow at the same rate. As a result, managers must rely on greater levels of technical expertise than ever before, and in our view, they must be more open to team and collaborative approaches to decision-making. One person simply cannot know enough to truly control every aspect of an organization's work.

In addition, the work environment has become more specialized, and the people at work have more diverse backgrounds. Managers must learn to understand the motivations of people from a wide variety of places and cultures. Since much of management's own work requires deploying resources as incentives to stimulate behavior, managers must learn about the culture and history of the people who work in their organizations. You can't motivate people unless you understand them.

Further, much of the communication and learning that takes place at work now occurs in informal and even social settings; these environments require care in navigating. The power relationship between staff and management remains in place even in social settings, and management must take great care in ensuring that staff do not feel abused.

Humor itself can be culturally bound, and what one person finds funny another person might well find insulting.[15] Some may lament the "loss of spontaneity" in the modern workplace, or argue against "political correctness," and we are not arguing against humor or informality; we are simply observing that old assumptions are based on a homogeneous environment that no longer exists. Managers must communicate and listen to their staff and seek to understand without making assumptions.

We have also learned that culture does not only differ by geography, but by generation itself. Baby boomers, members of Generation X, and millennials all grew up in different economic, social, political, and particularly technological environments. People our age did not grow up with the internet or social media. We can imagine a world without those resources. But millennials cannot. Thus, the use of, reliance on, and understanding of these communication and information technologies can differ by age. This, too, creates a distinction that a manager must understand. Differences across culture, geography, generation, field of knowledge, sexual orientation, gender identity, race, ethnicity, and personal history are to be expected. They form the character of the modern workplace.

Management based on emotion, "gut feeling," and misguided efforts to convey command should be replaced by decisions based on real-time performance data, give and take with staff, and discussion and learning in teams comprised of staff and management. This is a style designed to elicit maximum brain power and creativity.

THE FUTURE OF MANAGEMENT

Throughout history, families evolved into tribes, tribes into communities, communities into cities, and cities into modern sovereign nation-states. Throughout this evolution of social settings, political institutions, economic arrangements, and changing technologies, human biology and behavior remained stable. Many of our traits evolved over time and represent the survival of those traits that Darwin would have argued contributed most to our survival. We are genetically hardwired to act in the ways we act, and so even though we are emphasizing changes in work, workers, and management, this must all be viewed through a lens of relative stability.

Work will continue to change much faster than people will. As people, we still like to be recognized for our accomplishments, and we hope, in some ways, to be seen as unique and important; but we also want to be accepted by groups and have the sense that we "belong." The future of management requires that managers be agile enough to learn the new technologies and economic arrangements necessary to ensure their organizations produce the outcomes needed to generate resources.[16]

Learning, communication, listening, coordinating, and facilitating are far more important than envisioning, commanding, or controlling.

We are all surrounded by bad and inadequately trained managers. We see them in the private sector, in government, in nonprofits, and, of course, in universities too. Many people are better at selling themselves than at managing their organizations. In other instances, people are promoted to retain their technical expertise, but as they move up the hierarchy, they find that more and more people report to them—and despite their expertise, they do not know how to manage. These incompetent managers move from management position to management position, leaving organizational destruction in their wake. Because management is a craft and not a science, and today's world values science over craft, few take the time to apprentice and learn the craft. We don't really expect to see that change. In that respect, the future of management can be found in today's managers.

Nevertheless, we are compelled to write about management, and to teach and even practice it. While we may be surrounded by bad management and bad managers, we have both also worked for talented managers who have given pieces of their souls to build institutions. The presence of these brilliant managers convinces us that excellent management can be learned. One often hears that leaders are born and not made and that leadership is different and more important than management. In our view, leadership is part of the work of management, and leaders very much can be made through listening, observing, and learning. Inspired leadership is a part of effective management, and in our opinion, both are built on thoughtfulness, humility, and faith.

The two of us are "professors of practice" at Columbia. That is an academic position that has evolved during our time here, as more of our colleagues have come to understand the importance of thoughtful, reflective management practice. Both of us have managed organizations and served as management consultants. We have reflected on and written about effective management for over three decades. The goal of this book was to present our collective understanding of the practice of management.

To the highest extent possible, we have resisted our normal tendency to write and teach through analogy and case examples. When we use this book in management classes, however, we will separately present contemporary cases that help illuminate the concepts here. Indeed, the logic of a book like this is that it be used along with case studies, and we continue to believe strongly in the case method of teaching management. For this work, however, cases seem too time-bound to meet its objectives; but we believe the concepts presented will remain relevant even as case examples fade into history.

ACKNOWLEDGMENTS

STEVEN COHEN

I would like to acknowledge my good friend and long-time colleague, coauthor Bill Eimicke. Our shared understanding of organizations and public ethics has bound us together over decades of teaching and learning. I also acknowledge my professor of organization theory and EPA management mentor Marc Tipermas. Marc's brilliance in understanding organizations and business is unsurpassed, and many of the ideas in this book originated with him. I am grateful for the management lessons I learned from Ron Brand, former head of the U.S. Environmental Protection Agency's Office of Underground Storage Tanks (OUST) and my coauthor on a book about Total Quality Management (TQM) in government. I also thank Tom Brisbin and Mike Bieber of Willdan for teaching me, as their academic board member, how private firms are managed. I am indebted to Columbia colleagues George Sarrinikolaou, Kelsie DeFrancia, Dong Guo, Satyajit Bose, Alison Miller, Stephanie Hoyt, Maya Lugo, Kristie Stack, Louise Rosen, and Jeffrey Fralick. I am deeply grateful for the support of my family, my brilliant and loving wife Donna Fishman, my wonderful daughters Gabriella Rose and Ariel Mariah, their fantastic spouses and partners Eitan Grossbard and Rob Bowell, my perfect granddaughter Lily Bowell, and my stalwart siblings Judith, Robby, and Myra. The first manager I ever knew was my father Marvin, who was a corporate executive in the sixties and a corporation president in the early seventies. I have always felt that my mother would have run an organization had she not been denied access to college due to the casual sexism of her time. This book reflects some of the lessons of management and mismanagement I learned in their home on East 59th Street in Brooklyn a half a century ago.

BILL EIMICKE

I would like to acknowledge my friend, professional colleague, inspiration, and many-time coauthor Steven Cohen. Steve knows more about management and environmental policy than anyone on the planet, and I am fortunate that he called me to join his Columbia's School of International and Public Affairs advisory board more than thirty years ago. I am deeply grateful to Stephen Koff, who introduced me to political science at the Maxwell School. Congressperson Donna Shalala was truly a mentor and role model through my time in graduate school and my early years in politics. Dr. Shalala has shown us all that knowledge, hard work, and a deep commitment to compassion and empathy not only make the world a better place but can be done throughout various organizations and sectors.

Stephen Goldsmith, Steven Fulop, Chuck Todd, Michael Bloomberg, Sarah Bloom Raskin, Avril Haines, David Dinkins, and Milena Gomez Koff are colleagues, mentors, and friends who remind us all every day that one can make a difference in today's highly politicized world without compromising civility or integrity.

Most important, I thank my wife, Karen Murphy, from whom I have learned so much about melding the power of intellect with the strength to never stop fighting for what is right—no matter how high the mountain or how formidable the evil.

We would like to acknowledge our debt to Tanya Heikkila who joined us as coauthor on several editions of *The Effective Public Manager* and shared her many insights on management fundamentals. We are also indebted to our friend and colleague Ester Fuchs, who continues to demonstrate how one applies academic knowledge to the practice of public policy. We would also like to thank the book's copy editor, Lynn Everett, as well as our senior editor, Stephen Wesley, and his entire team at Columbia University Press. We are grateful for the leaders of Columbia University who provided us with the time and resources we needed to complete this work: President Lee Bollinger, former Provost John Coatsworth, Dean Merit Janow, and Dean Jason Wingard. Columbia is a great university and we are proud to have been part of it for many years.

NOTES

1. THE EVOLUTION OF MANAGEMENT

1. Frederick Winslow Taylor, *The Principles of Scientific Management* (New York: Harper & Brothers, 1911).
2. "Scientific Management," *The Economist,* February 9, 2009, https://www.economist.com/node/13092819.
3. "W. Edwards Deming: Total Quality Management Thinker," British Library, 2009, https://www.bl.uk/people/w-edwards -deming.
4. "Frederick Winslow Taylor: Father of Scientific Management Thinker," British Library, 2009, https://www.bl.uk/people /frederick-winslow-taylor.
5. "Elton Mayo: The Hawthorne Experiments Thinker," British Library, 2018, https://www.bl.uk/people/elton-mayo.
6. Chester Barnard, *The Functions of the Executive* (Cambridge, MA: Harvard University Press, 1938).
7. Philip Selznick. *Leadership in Administration: A Sociological Interpretation* (Evanston, IL: Row, Peterson, 1957).
8. Peter Drucker. *Concept of the Corporation.* (New York: John Day, 1946); Peter Drucker, *The Practice of Management* (New York: Harper & Row, 1954).
9. Thomas J. Peters and Robert H. Waterman. *In Search of Excellence: Lessons from America's Best-Run Companies* (New York: Harper & Row, 1982).

10. "Management by Walking About," *The Economist*, September 8, 2009, https://www.economist.com/node/12075015.
11. "What We Do," U.S. Securities and Exchange Commission, June 10, 2013, https://www.sec.gov/Article/whatwedo.html.
12. "Joseph P. Kennedy," John F. Kennedy Presidential Library and Museum, https://www.jfklibrary.org/learn/about-jfk/the-kennedy-family/joseph-p-kennedy; David Nasaw, interview by David Davies, "Joseph Kennedy, 'Patriarch' of an American Dynasty," December 12, 2012, https://www.npr.org/2012/12/12/166488040/joseph-kennedy-patriarch-of-an-american-dynasty.
13. "What We Do," *U.S. Securities and Exchange Commission*, June 10, 2013. Accessed June 5, 2018, https://www.sec.gov/Article/whatwedo.html.
14. James F. Strother, "The Establishment of Generally Accepted Accounting Principles and Generally Accepted Auditing Standards," *Vanderbilt Law Review* (1975): 201–233.
15. Brian Detlor, "Information Management," *International Journal of Information Management* (2010): 103–108, doi:10.1016/j.ijinfomgt.2009.12.001.
16. Kevin J. Laverty, "Economic 'Short-Termism': The Debate, the Unresolved Issues, and the Implications for Management Practice and Research," *Academy of Management Review* 21, no. 3 (1996): 825–860, http://www.jstor.org/stable/259003.
17. Kent Bauer, "KPIs—the Metrics That Drive Performance Management," *DM Review* 14, no. 9 (September 2004): 63, http://ezproxy.cul.columbia.edu/login?url=https://search.proquest.com/docview/214675051?accountid=10226.
18. "Just-in-Time," *The Economist*, July 6, 2009, https://www.economist.com/node/13976392.
19. "Supply-Chain Management," *The Economist*, April 6, 2009, https://www.economist.com/node/13432670.
20. Todd Dewett and Gareth R. Jones, "The Role of Information Technology in the Organization: A Review, Model, and Assessment," *Journal of Management* 27, no. 3 (June 2001).
21. Albert Park, Gaurav Nayyar, and Patrick Low, *Supply Chain Perspectives and Issues: A Literature Review* (Switzerland: WTO Publications, Fung Global Institute, 2013).

2. LEADERSHIP

22. Douglas M. Lambert and Martha C. Cooper. "Issues in Supply Chain Management," *Industrial Marketing Management* 29, no. 1 (January 2000): 65–83; John T. Mentzer and Ila Manuj. "Global Supply Chain Risk Management Strategies," *International Journal of Physical Distribution & Logistics Management* 38, no. 3 (April 2008): 192–223.

23. John Morelli, "Environmental Sustainability: A Definition for Environmental Professionals," *Journal of Environmental Sustainability* (2001): 1–9.

24. Peter Drucker, *Management: Tasks, Responsibilities, Practices* (New York: HarperCollins, 2009).

25. Phillip Selznick, *Leadership in Administration: A Sociological Interpretation* (New York: Row, Peterson, 1957).

2. LEADERSHIP

1. Max Weber, *The Three Types of Legitimate Rule,* trans. Hans Gerth and Max Rheinstein, vol. 4 (Berkeley, CA: Berkeley Publications in Society and Institutions, 1958).

2. Reinhard Bendix, *Max Weber: An Intellectual Portrait* (Berkeley: University of California Press, 1977).

3. Bendix, *Max Weber.*

4. Weber, *Three Types of Legitimate Rule.*

5. Dennis W. Organ, "Leadership: The Great Man Theory Revisited," *Business Horizons*, 39, no. 3: 1–4.

6. Weber, *Three Types of Legitimate Rule.*

7. Peter F. Drucker, *Management: Tasks, Responsibilities, Practices* (New York: HarperBusiness, 1993).

8. Steve A. Cohen, "Defining and Measuring Effectiveness in Public Management," *Public Productivity and Management Review*, 17, no. 1, https://doi.org/10.2307/3381048.

9. Peter F. Drucker, *The Daily Drucker: 366 Days of Insight and Motivation for Getting the Right Thing Done* (New York: HarperBusiness, 2004).

10. James M. Burns, *Leadership* (New York: HarperCollins, 1978).

11. Burns, *Leadership.*

12. Burns, *Leadership*.
13. Doris K. Goodwin, *Leadership in Turbulent Times* (New York: Simon & Schuster, 2018).
14. Warren Bennis and Burt Nanus, *Leaders: Strategies for Taking Charge* (New York: HarperCollins, 2007).
15. Bennis and Nanus, *Leaders*.
16. Burns, *Leadership*.
17. Ovidiu I. Dobre, "Employee Motivation and Organizational Performance," *Review of Applied Socio-Economic Research* 5, no.1: 53–60.
18. Burns, *Leadership*.
19. Burns, *Leadership*.
20. Buffett and Eimicke, *Social Value Investing*.
21. Joseph W. Pfiefer, "Crisis Leadership: The Art of Adapting to Extreme Events," *Harvard Kennedy School: Program on Crisis Leadership* (2013): 24.
22. Pfiefer, "Crisis Leadership."
23. Goodwin, *Leadership in Turbulent Times*.

3. BUDGET, MANAGEMENT, AND CONTROL

1. A. Khan and W. B. Hildreth, *Budget Theory in the Public Sector* (Westport, CT: Greenwood Publishing Group, 2002).

4. HOW WORK GETS DONE: HUMAN RESOURCE MANAGEMENT, ORGANIZATION STRUCTURE, AND STANDARD OPERATING PROCEDURES

1. Pamela Hinds and Sara Kiesler, *Distributed Work* (Cambridge, MA: MIT Press, 2002).
2. Gerald Friedman, "Workers without Employers: Shadow Corporations and the Rise of the Gig Economy," *Review of Keynesian Economics* 2, no. 2: 171–188, https://doi.org/10.4337/roke.2014.02.03.
3. Mirjana Radović Marković, "Managing the Organizational Change and Culture in the Age of Globalization," *Journal of*

Business Economics and Management 9, no. 1 (2008): 3–11, doi: 10.3846/1611-1699.2008.9.3–11.

4. Jonas Prising, "Four Changes Shaping the Labour Market," *World Economic Forum.* Accessed June 11, 2018, https://www.weforum .org/agenda/2016/01/four-changes-shaping-the-labour-market/.

5. Neal Chalofsky, "An Emerging Construct for Meaningful Work," *Human Resource Development International* 6, no. 1 (March 2003): 69–83.

6. Brent A. Scott, Jason A. Colquitt, E. Layne Paddock, and Timothy A. Judge, *A Daily Investigation of the Role of Manager Empathy on Employee Well-Being,* vol. 113 (Amsterdam: Elsevier, 2010).

7. "W. Edwards Deming: Total Quality Management Thinker," *British Library.* Accessed June 4, 2018, https://www.bl.uk/people /w-edwards-deming.

8. Tomas Chamorro-Premuzic, "Does Money Really Affect Motivation? A Review of the Research," *Harvard Business Review*, August 07, 2014. Accessed June 11, 2018, https://hbr.org/2013/04/does -money-really-affect-motiv.

9. "Law Enforced by EEOC," *U.S. Equal Employment Opportunity Commission.* Accessed June 11, 2018, https://www.eeoc.gov/laws /statutes/.

10. Kenneth W. Foster, "Organization Theory," *Encyclopedia Britannica.* April 22, 2016. Accessed June 12, 2018, https://www.britan nica.com/topic/organization-theory.

11. R. E. Kraut, R. S. Fish, R. W. Root, and B. L. Chalfonte, "Informal Communication in Organizations: Form, Function, and Technology," *Groupware and Computer-Supported Cooperative Work* (1993): 287–314.

12. Marcia W. Blenko, Michael C. Mankins, and Paul Rogers, "The Key to Successful Corporate Reorganization," *Forbes.* July 30, 2010. Accessed July 12, 2018, https://www.forbes.com/2010/07/30 /corporate-reorganization-abb-ford-leadership-managing-bain .html#3ff707486812.

5. HOW WE KNOW WHAT'S BEEN DONE: ORGANIZATIONAL PERFORMANCE AND INFORMATION MANAGEMENT

1. Steven Cohen, William Eimicke, and Tanya Heikkila, *The Effective Public Manager,* 5th ed. (San Francisco: Jossey-Bass, 2013), 259.
2. Robert S. Kaplan and David P. Norton, *The Balanced Scorecard* (Boston, MA: Harvard Business School Press, 1996), 208–249.
3. Peter Drucker (with Joseph A. Maciariello), *Daily Drucker* (New York: Harper Business, 2004), 295.
4. Drucker and Maciariello, *Daily Drucker,* 292.
5. Drucker and Maciariello, *Daily Drucker,* 293.
6. Drucker and Maciariello, *Daily Drucker,* 294.
7. Kaplan and Norton, *Balanced Scorecard.*
8. Kaplan and Norton, *Balanced Scorecard,* 21–166.
9. We are grateful for insights on managing information and communications technologies for the common good offered by Robert Z. Tumin, SIPA adjunct professor of international and public affairs at Columbia University and former deputy commissioner of the NYPD.
10. Kai-Fu Lee, *AI Super-Powers—China, Silicon Valley and the New World Order* (New York: Houghton, Mifflin Harcourt, 2018), 1–21.
11. Kai-Fu Lee, 13–15 and 107–139.
12. Howard W. Buffett and William B. Eimicke, *Social Value Investing—A Management Framework for Effective Partnerships* (New York: Columbia University Press, 2018), 4–5.
13. A more detailed list of these tools and methodologies, along with their advantages and limitations, can be found in Buffett and Eimicke, *Social Value Investing,* 257–281.
14. For more information and references on this subject, see Buffett and Eimicke, *Social Value Investing,* 257–265.
15. Buffett and Eimicke, *Social Value Investing,* 265–281.

6. SUSTAINABILITY AND MATERIAL MANAGEMENT

1. Paul Shrivastava, "The Role of Corporations in Achieving Ecological Sustainability," *Academy of Management Review* 20, no. 4 (1995): 936, doi:10.2307/258961.
2. G. H. Brundtland, *Our Common Future: Report of the World Commission on Environment and Development* (New York: Oxford University Press, 1987).
3. Steven Cohen, *Sustainability Management* (New York: Columbia University Press, 2014).
4. Paul Simon, "There Goes Rhymin' Simon," 2011, Columbia/Legacy B004MRX8A6, compact disc.
5. United Nations Department of Economic and Social Affairs, *World Economic and Social Survey 2013: Sustainability Development Challenges* (New York: United Nations, 2013).
6. Clay Shirky, "The Political Power of Social Media: Technology, the Public Sphere, and Political Change," *Foreign Affairs* 90, no. 1 (2011): 28–41, http://www.jstor.org/stable/25800379.
7. Johan Rockström, Will Steffen, Kevin Noone, et al., "Planetary Boundaries: Exploring the Safe Operating Space for Humanity," *Ecology and Society* 14, no. 2 (2009), http://www.jstor.org/stable/26268316.
8. National Research Council, *The Role of Technology in Environmentally Sustainable Development* (Washington, DC: National Academies Press, 1995).
9. Sheila Bonini, Stephan Gorner, and Alissa Jones, "How Companies Manage Sustainability: McKinsey Global Survey Results," *McKinsey & Company*, March 2010. Accessed June 19, 2018, https://www.mckinsey.com/business-functions/sustainability-and-resource-productivity/our-insights/how-companies-manage-sustainability-mckinsey-global-survey-results; Deborah E. de Lange, Timo Busch, and Javier Delgado-Ceballos, "Sustaining Sustainability in Organizations," *Journal of Business Ethics* 110, no. 2 (2012): 151–156.
10. Manuela Weber, *The Business Case for Corporate Social Responsibility: A Company-Level Measurement Approach For CSR*, vol. 26 (Lüneburg: Elsevier, 2008).

11. Hayley Tsukayama, "The Rise of the Chief Information Officer," *Washington Post*. September 22, 2015. Accessed June 20, 2018, https://www.washingtonpost.com/news/on-leadership/wp/2015/09/22/the-rise-of-the-chief-information-officer/?noredirect=on&utm_term=.09b7e5dd54d9.

7. STRATEGIC PLANNING

1. Richard F. Vancil and Peter Lorange, "Strategic Planning in Diversified Companies," *Harvard Business Review,* January 1975.
2. U.S. Department of Agriculture, Risk Management Agency, *SWOT Analysis: A Tool for Making Better Business Decisions* (Washington, DC: U.S. Department of Agriculture, Risk Management Agency, 2008).
3. Martyn Pitt and Dimitrios Koufopoulos, "Enterprise Stakeholders, Identity, and Purpose," in *Essentials of Strategic Management* (London: SAGE Publications, 2012), 98–123, doi: 10.4135/978 1526435736.n4.
4. Michael T. Hannan, "Organizational Analysis," *Encyclopedia Britannica,* November 19, 2015, https://www.britannica.com/science/organizational-analysis.
5. Catherine A. Maritan and Gwendolyn K. Lee, "Resource Allocation and Strategy," *Journal of Management* 43 (8): 2411–2420, doi:10.1177/0149206317729738.
6. A. Neely, M. Gregory, and K. Platts, "Performance Measurement System Design: A Literature Review and Research Agenda," *International Journal of Operations and Production Management,* 25 (12): 1228–1263, http://ezproxy.cul.columbia.edu/login?url=https://search.proquest.com/docview/232323050?accountid=10226.
7. Howard Distelzweig and Connie Clark, "Strategic Formulation," *Encyclopedia of Strategy Formulation,* http://www.referenceforbusiness.com/management/Sc-Str/Strategy-Formulation.html.
8. Scott Edinger, "Three Cs of Implementing Strategy," *Forbes,* August 7, 2012.

9. Howard Distelzweig and Connie Clark, "Strategic Formulation," *Encyclopedia of Strategy Formulation,* http://www.reference forbusiness.com/management/Sc-Str/Strategy-Formulation .html.
10. Sally Blount and Shana Carrol, "Overcome Resistance to Change with Two Conversations," *Harvard Business Review,* May 16, 2017.

8. CONTRACTS, OUTSOURCING, SUPPLY CHAINS, AND THE MAKE-OR-BUY DECISION

1. "What Is Performance-Based Contracting?" *World Health Organization,* http://www.who.int/management/resources/finances /Section2-3.pdf.
2. "Importance of Contract Management," eSupport KPO, http:// www.esupportkpo.com/images/Learning%20Pages%20-%20 Articles%20%20Importance%20of%20Contract%20Management.pdf.
3. Kristian Jaakkola, "A Way to Successful and Strategic Contract Management," Efecte Corp, http://www.icoste.org/NORDNET 2004%20Papers/Jaakkola.pdf.
4. *Managing Conflict of Interest in the Public Sector: A Toolkit* (Paris: OECD Publishing, 2005), https://doi.org/10.1787/9789264018 242-en.
5. Roman Belotserkovskiy, Britta Lietke, Jayant Sewak, and Adina Teodorian, "Contracting for Performance: Unlocking Additional Value," *McKinsey,* https://www.mckinsey.com/business-functions /operations/our-insights/contracting-for-performance -unlocking-additional-value.
6. "Other Transactions Guide for Prototype Projects," U.S. Department of Defense, https://www.darpa.mil/attachments/OTGuide PrototypeProjects.pdf.
7. Gian Luigi Albano and Marco Sparro, "Flexible Strategies for Centralized Public Procurement," *Review of Economics and Institutions* 1, no. 2 (October 2010), https://papers.ssrn.com/sol3/papers .cfm?abstract_id=1887791.

8. Sandy Allen and Ashok Chandrashekar, *Outsourcing Services: The Contract Is Just the Beginning*, vol. 43 (Amsterdam: Elsevier Advanced Technology Publications, 2000).

9. Peter K. Murdock, "The New Reality of Employee Loyalty," *Forbes*, https://www.forbes.com/sites/forbeshumanresourcescoun cil/2017/12/28/the-new-reality-of-employee-loyalty/#255144 da4cf3.

10. Tim Bajarin, "How Lenovo Became a Global PC Powerhouse after IBM Deal," *Time*, May 4, 2015. Accessed July 25, 2018, http://time.com/3845674/lenovo-ibm/; Bridget van Kralingen, "IBM's Transformation—from Survival to Success," *Forbes*, 2010, https://www.forbes.com/2010/07/07/ibm-transformation -lessons-leadership-managing-change.html#dd734e23afbd.

11. Chester Barnard, *The Functions of the Executive* (Cambridge, MA: Harvard University Press, 1938).

9. CROSS-SECTOR PARTNERSHIPS: HOW THE THREE SECTORS DIFFER AND WHY COLLABORATION IS BENEFICIAL

1. Steven. A. Cohen, William B. Eimicke, and Tanya Heikkila, *The Effective Public Manager*, 4th ed. (San Francisco, CA: Jossey-Bass, 2008).

2. William. E. Leuchtenburg, "Franklin D. Roosevelt: Domestic Affairs," October 4, 2016. Accessed January 22, 2019, https://miller center.org/president/fdroosevelt/domestic-affairs.

3. Richard. F. Weingroff, "Federal-Aid Highway Act of 1956: Creating the Interstate System," *Public Roads*, 60 (1), Summer 1996, https://www.fhwa.dot.gov/publications/publicroads/96summer/p96 su10.cfm

4. Howard. W. Buffett and William. B. Eimicke, *Social Value Investing: A Management Framework for Effective Partnerships* (New York: Columbia University Press, 2018); Steven. A. Cohen and William. B. Eimicke, *The Responsible Contract Manager* (Washington, DC: Georgetown University Press, 2006).

10. MARKETING, STAKEHOLDERS, AND PUBLIC ENGAGEMENT

5. Buffett and Eimicke, *Social Value Investing*.

6. David Smith and Jeanine Becker, "The Essential Skills of Cross-Sector Leadership," *Stanford Social Innovation* Review, Winter 2018. Accessed January 22, 2019, https://ssir.org/articles/entry/the_essential_skills_of_cross_sector_leadership.

7. Stephen Goldsmith and Neil Kleiman, *A New City O/S: The Power of Open, Collaborative, and Distributed Governance* (Washington, DC: Brookings Institution, 2017).

8. James Rosewell, "Performance Optimization: Techniques and Strategies," *Smashing Magazine*, 2014, https://shop.smashingmagazine.com/products/performance-optimization-techniques-and-strategies.

10. MARKETING, STAKEHOLDER RELATIONS, AND PUBLIC ENGAGEMENT: IMPROVING MANAGEMENT COMMUNICATIONS

1. H. H. Gerth and C. Wright Mills, eds., *From Max Weber: Essays in Sociology* (New York: Oxford University Press, 1946), 43, 78–80, 295–296.

2. Peter Drucker, *The Essential Drucker* (New York: HarperBusiness, 2004).

3. A very accessible introduction to marketing is Allan Dib's *The 1-Page Marketing Plan* (New York: Successwise, 2018).

4. Brandingmag, "What Is Branding and Why Is It Important for Your Business?" Accessed March 9, 2019, https://www.brandingmag.com/2015/10/14/what-is-branding-and-why-is-it-important-for-your-business/.

5. See Donald Miller, *Building a Brand Story* (New York: HarperCollins Leadership, 2017).

6. Farzana Parveen Tajudeen, Noor Ismawati Jaafar, and Sulaiman Ainin, "Understanding the Impact of Social Media Usage among Organizations," *Information & Management,* 55 (2018): 308–332, http://d.doi.org/10.1016/j.im.2017.08.004.

10. MARKETING, STAKEHOLDERS, AND PUBLIC ENGAGEMENT

7. See K. N. C., "Shirky Squares the Circle," *The Economist,* Politics and the Internet, January 5, 2011, https://www.economist.com/babbage/2011/01/05/shirky-squares-the-circle.

8. The best book we have found that focuses on all three skills is Joann Baney's *Guide to Interpersonal Communication* (Upper Saddle River, NJ: Prentice Hall Pearson, 2004).

9. We find Daniel Shapiro's *Negotiating the Nonnegotiable* (New York: Viking, 2016) and Roger Fisher and William Ury's *Getting to Yes* (New York: Penguin Books, 1991) to be extremely valuable resources on this topic.

10. Shapiro, *Negotiating the Nonnegotiable,* xv–xvi; 131–206.

11. Myria W. Allen and Robert M. Brady, "Total Quality Management, Organizational Commitment, Perceived Organizational Support, and Intraorganizational Communication," *Management Communication Quarterly* 10, no. 3 (February 1997): 316–341.

12. Kyoung Ja Kim, Jung Sook Han, Mi Sook Seo, Bong Hee Jang, Mi Mi Park, Hyeoung Mi Ham, and Moon Sook Yoo, "Relationship Between Intra-Organizational Communication Satisfaction and Safety Attitude of Nurses," *Journal of Korean Academy of Nursing Administration,* June 13, 2012, https://jkana.or.kr.

13. We highly recommend Bruce Berger, "Employee/Organizational Communications," Institute for Public Relations, November 17, 2008, https://instituteforpr.org/employee-organizational-communications/.

11. ORGANIZATIONAL ETHICS

1. Lynn S. Paine, "Managing for Organizational Integrity," *Harvard Business Review,* March-April 1994, https://hbr.org/1994/03/managing-for-organizational-integrity.

2. John Stuart Mill, *Utilitarianism,* 2nd ed. (Indianapolis, IN: Hackett Publishing Company, 2001).

3. John Rawls, *A Theory of Justice* (Cambridge, MA: Belknap Press of Harvard University Press, 1971).

4. United Nations Declaration of Human Rights. Accessed March 29, 2019, https://www.un.org/en/universal-declaration-human -rights.

5. Organizational ethics is a broad and complicated area that requires much more coverage than can be covered in a short chapter. To learn more, we recommend Craig E. Johnson, *Organizational Ethics—A Practical Approach* (Los Angeles, CA: Sage Publications, 2012).

6. Transparency International, "What Is Corruption?" Accessed on March 28, 2019, https://www.transparency.org/what-is-corrup tion#define.

7. For some examples of how this can work, see Steven Cohen, *The Sustainable City* (New York: Columbia University Press, 2017).

12. THE FUTURE OF WORK: HOW WILL CHANGES IN WORK AND SOCIETY CHANGE MANAGEMENT?

1. Tasnim B. Kazi, "Effects of Globalization on Work and Organizations: Exploring Post-Industrialism, Post-Fordism, Work and Management in the Global Era," *Inquiries Journal/Student Pulse* 3 (12), http://www.inquiriesjournal.com/a?id=1693.

2. Central Intelligence Agency, *The World Factbook*, 1957, https:// www.cia.gov/library/publications/the-world-factbook/fields /2012.html.

3. James Manyika, "What Is the Future of Work?" *New World of Work,* podcast audio, December 2017, https://www.mckinsey.com /featured-insights/future-of-organizations-and-work/what-is -the-future-of-work.

4. Rajiv Bhandari, "Impact of Technology on Logistics and Supply Chain Management," *IOSR Journal of Business and Management* 2, pp. 29–32, http://www.iosrjournals.org/iosr-jbm/papers/7th -ibrc-volume-2/19.pdf.

5. Josh Bersin, "The Future of Work: It's Already Here—and Not as Scary as You Think," *Forbes*, September 2016, https://www.forbes

.com/sites/joshbersin/2016/09/21/the-future-of-work-its-already
-here-and-not-as-scary-as-you-think/#48b74d194bf5.

6. Graham Wilkinson, Ian Brooks, and Jamie Weatherson, *The International Business Environment*, 2nd ed. (n.p.: Financial Times
Prentice Hall, 2010), https://catalogue.pearsoned.co.uk/assets/hip
/gb/hip_gb_pearsonhighered/samplechapter/Brooksch9.pdf.

7. James Manyika, "Technology, Jobs, and the Future of Work,"
McKinsey Global Institute, February 2017, https://www.mckinsey
.com/featured-insights/employment-and-growth/technology
-jobs-and-the-future-of-work.

8. Caleb Gayle, "U.S. Gig Economy: Data Shows 16m People in
'Contingent or Alternative' Work," *The Guardian,* June 2018,
https://www.theguardian.com/business/2018/jun/07/america
-gig-economy-work-bureau-labor-statistics.

9. The Council on Economic Advisors, "Work-Life Balance and the
Economics of Workplace Flexibility," Executive Office of the President of the United States, June 2014, https://obamawhitehouse
.archives.gov/sites/default/files/docs/updated_workplace_flex
_report_final_0.pdf.

10. Karl Moore and Kyle Hill, "The Decline but Not Fall of
Hierarchy—What Young People Really Want," *Forbes,* June 2011,
https://www.forbes.com/sites/karlmoore/2011/06/14/the
-decline-but-not-fall-of-hierarchy-what-young-people-really
-want/#534af0e45843.

11. Yossi Sheffi and James Blayney Rice Jr., "A Supply Chain View of
the Resilient Enterprise," *MIT Sloan Management Review* 47, no. 1
(September 2005), https://www.researchgate.net/publication/2555
99289_A_Supply_Chain_View_of_the_Resilient_Enterprise.

12. Bersin, "The Future of Work."

13. Ed Batista, "Happy Workaholics Need Boundaries, Not Balance,"
Harvard Business Review, December 6, 2013, https://hbr.org/2013
/12/happy-workaholics-need-boundaries-not-balance.

14. John Stuckey and David White, "When and When Not to Vertically Integrate," *McKinsey Quarterly*, August 1993, https://
www.mckinsey.com/business-functions/strategy-and-corporate
-finance/our-insights/when-and-when-not-to-vertically
-integrate.

15. Roger Trapp, "Why Successful Leaders Acknowledge Cultural Differences," *Forbes,* June 2014, https://www.forbes.com/sites/rogertrapp/2014/06/30/why-successful-leaders-acknowledge-cultural-differences/#1f2174f3661f.

16. "The Agile Manager," *McKinsey Quarterly,* July 2018, https://www.mckinsey.com/business-functions/organization/our-insights/the-agile-manager.

INDEX

INDEX

INDEX

supply chains, global: development of, 13; and human resources management, increased challenges of, 14, 53–54; management changes driven by, 13–14, 166; and specialization, 14

sustainability: effect on management practices, 14–15; as ethical imperative, 159–160; policies needed to attain, 84; technology needed to attain, 83–84

sustainability management: changes necessary to implement, 84–85; and changing needs, monitoring of, 86; cost reductions resulting from, 82–83; definition of, 82; as efficiency maximization, 82–83, 85, 89–90; as essential to good management, 82, 90; integration into routine operations, 87–88; knowledge and skills needed by managers in, 86–87, 88–89; and ongoing evolution of manager's role, 82; organizational form, 88; origin of concept, 82, 89; rationale for, 82–83; steps toward implementation of, 85–86

SWOT (strengths, weaknesses, opportunities, and threats) analysis, in strategic planning, 94

Taylor, Fredrick Winslow, 7, 146

Taylorism, 7

team management approach, in cross-sector partnerships, 126–127

technology, new: and changing nature of work, 165; as cost-reduction measure, 45–46. *See also* information technology improvements

theory-of-change logic model, in development of cross-sector partnership, 124–125

Total Quality Management (TQM), 8, 55, 145–146

TQM. *See* Total Quality Management

training, ongoing: for crisis response, 29, 33; leaders' role in ensuring, 29

transparency in hiring, and equal opportunity, 155–156

United Nations Declaration of Human Rights, 151

United Nations World Health Organization, 79

utilitarianism, and organizational ethics, 150, 151

value-chain analysis, in development of cross-sector partnership, 124–125

Lightning Source UK Ltd.
Milton Keynes UK
UKHW011824120622
404261UK00002B/106